D1564282

Born
to Lead

Born to Lead

Unlock the Magnificence in Yourself and Others

Bill Lamond

ALPHA

A member of Penguin Group (USA) Inc.

ALPHA BOOKS

Published by the Penguin Group

Penguin Group (USA) Inc., 375 Hudson Street, New York, New York 10014, U.S.A.

Penguin Group (Canada), 10 Alcorn Avenue, Toronto, Ontario, Canada M4V 3B2 (a division of Pearson Penguin Canada Inc.)

Penguin Books Ltd, 80 Strand, London WC2R 0RL, England

Penguin Ireland, 25 St Stephen's Green, Dublin 2, Ireland (a division of Penguin Books Ltd)

Penguin Group (Australia), 250 Camberwell Road, Camberwell, Victoria 3124, Australia (a division of Pearson Australia Group Pty Ltd)

Penguin Books India Pvt Ltd, 11 Community Centre, Panchsheel Park, New Delhi—110 017, India

Penguin Group (NZ), cnr Airborne and Rosedale Roads, Albany, Auckland 1310, New Zealand (a division of Pearson New Zealand Ltd)

Penguin Books (South Africa) (Pty) Ltd, 24 Sturdee Avenue, Rosebank, Johannesburg 2196, South Africa

Penguin Books Ltd, Registered Offices: 80 Strand, London WC2R 0RL, England

Copyright © 2006 by Bill Lamond

International Standard Book Number: 1-59257-559-5

Library of Congress Catalog Card Number: 2006929098

08   07   06   8   7   6   5   4   3   2   1

Interpretation of the printing code: The rightmost number of the first series of numbers is the year of the book's printing; the rightmost number of the second series of numbers is the number of the book's printing. For example, a printing code of 06-1 shows that the first printing occurred in 2006.

Printed in the United States of America

Most Alpha books are available at special quantity discounts for bulk purchases for sales promotions, premiums, fund-raising, or educational use. Special books, or book excerpts, can also be created to fit specific needs.

For details, write: Special Markets, Alpha Books, 375 Hudson Street, New York, NY 10014.

For my mother, Alice
and
Diane, Shion, and Maris

Contents

Introduction:
The New Feminine Principle

Born to lead? Yes, you are, even if you hold no political office and are not the president of an international business conglomerate. Like it or not, on top of a mate, kids, a house, and a career to care for, you have a new assignment—to save the world by ensuring that it goes on for your children and grandchildren. The bad news is that men are not going to do it. (I think you already know that.) The good news is that it is up to you personally and individually. You are part of a generation of women who will cast the deciding vote on the viability of the human race.

You have to devise, along with 3.2 billion other women and girls, a new strategy that revolutionizes the way all of us think and stops the wholesale destruction of this magnificent planet we live on. Fortunately, you don't have to go anywhere. There are no extra meetings to attend. You can do everything you need to do inside yourself and lead from wherever you are. Simply start with The Feminine Principle, which you live with every single day, then take a stand for a life in which you are a first-class, fully nourished person, with a voice for the visions and desires that every woman holds dear, and be that person everywhere you go. This is a time to shine in all your greatness. This book will show you how.

Ask yourself, "What is The Feminine Principle?" If you are like most people, you might think of the ways women act and what is important to them. Things like relationship, family, beauty, kindness, love, and grace might come to mind, as well as the way women walk and talk and gesture—what you might call the culture of being a woman. You might also think of the

Goddess-worship culture, where The Feminine Principle is another name for the feminine face of God.

There is a third possible answer, but it is invisible to most people. This third answer is the core of this book. It is my premise that The Feminine Principle, like all human ideas, is *a system of beliefs* about who and what women are and about their role in human affairs. This system of beliefs (or model), with its attendant roles, is automatically taught to girls as *what it is* to be female. These beliefs might have nothing to do with physically being female. More importantly, they might have nothing to do with what is in the best interest of women—or even of men.

The first goal of this book is to help you understand how The Feminine Principle works as a model of human behavior, so that you can change it as you see fit. When you start changing your belief systems for your greatest happiness, pleasure, and effectiveness, you literally become a world leader, because in pioneering a new world for yourself, you also make a new reality available for everyone around you.

The second goal is to identify four critical elements that are missing from The Feminine Principle for most women because of the way they learned it, and to give you the thinking and tools to claim them. When you add these elements—namely, Capacity, Truth, Voice, and Stance—into The Feminine Principle, you become whole and fulfilled. You become a "woman of greatness" who: (1) develops full Capacity for life and leadership by nourishing herself and others; (2) moves beyond old beliefs about being second class and tells the Truth about herself and the world; (3) has a clear Voice for her visions, appetites, and desires; and (4) takes her Stand for the world she wants, as a unique individual in her own right (regardless of relationships she might have). Such a woman embraces her real genius—the power to enhance rather than destroy.

These four elements are the keys to a New Feminine Principle. When you make them a part of your belief system, you create a brand-new set of beliefs about being feminine that elevates your status as a human being and makes real change in the world available. You also discover that The New Feminine Principle is really The Principle of Wholeness.

Waking Up to a New World

Fifteen years ago, I had an epiphany, a sudden opening of my reality that catapulted me into a brand-new world and changed everything about my view of women and men. To my utter amazement, the very first thing I noticed after this epiphany was that I could understand clearly what the women around me were talking about. I witnessed a degree of clarity, complexity, and richness in the way women think and speak that astounded me.

Perhaps the most profound realization I had was that women live in a world where standard logic, a mental approach to life, is not the prevailing mindset. More precisely, women live in a world that is a-logical rather than illogical; it is a world where sudden leaps occur that transcend logic and open new vistas. Women include logic when it is useful, but are no more bound by it than quantum physicists are bound by Newton's early theories about gravity. As one woman mentor of mine put it, "Men live in a cause-and-effect world. Everything must be explained and accounted for. Women live in a world of magic and miracle. We are not trying to control the world we live in. We want to cooperate with it."

Women live in a world that is more closely allied to chaos theory, where at any moment a whole new condition can arise and a new choice can be made. Ironically, the same men who can see the intellectual genius of chaos theory are often annoyed when women actually put it into practice.

The world of women's thinking and communication is more complex and subtle than that of the world of men. Gesture, tone, body posture, feeling, energy, and emotion are as important as what is said. Sometimes, what a woman omits from conversation is more important than what she does say. This comes from the fact that women have traditionally been suppressed and have had to develop more complex and subtle ways of communicating. It might also come from the fact that women are generally more open than men, and are therefore able to express at many levels simultaneously and take in large amounts of interrelated information as they speak. Women, by necessity, open themselves to express their sexuality and to give birth. The very fact of opening might be a crucial determinant of the energetic richness in which women live because it allows them to feel completely normal operating as an open system.

To my great surprise, I have discovered that I can switch back and forth between the masculine and feminine styles to take advantage of what each offers, and I am even able to merge them. I live nearly full-time in The Feminine Principle, not because I desire to be a woman—I really enjoy being a man—but because it gives me more of what I am looking for. In the world of women's thinking, there is deep relationship; global, nonlinear thinking; creativity; sensuality; a sense of something bigger to which I am connected; and playfulness. Like a person who owns two homes, I also live in the world of men's thinking when I want to make clear decisions and demarcations; when I require time and attention for myself; and when I want to simplify information.

After fifteen years of this journey, it is clear to me that both aspects live in me and that I require both to be whole. We come from parents of both genders and have an inheritance that is female and male. To cut ourselves off from one or the other sentences us to a life where our sense of wholeness can only be achieved by finding what we think we are missing in someone else. The New Feminine Principle is a model that allows us to combine the strengths of the feminine and masculine models to become whole, while sidestepping the pitfalls in each model that get in the way of fulfillment.

The Challenge of Leadership

For the last fifteen years, I have championed a new style of leadership that has the power to generate a world where we would all be happy to live. It has been my pleasure to train and coach hundreds of women and men to use this new thinking and style to develop personal strategies that give them more of what they want. Naturally, women learn this model more easily, because it starts from the feminine belief that everything is connected; however, they also have a hard time extricating themselves from the downside of the feminine model as it is culturally taught to them. Because leadership outside the home has been the traditional territory of men, women often buy into men's evaluation of them, which is based on men's beliefs about leadership.

It has been more challenging to teach this way of thinking to men. When men open themselves to women's perceptual point of view, they experience an almost immediate, overwhelming fear, often articulated as "not wanting to be like a woman." This fear of emasculation is real and powerful, though it has no basis in fact.

Though the jury is still out, it might be that men past a certain age will never to able to use The New Feminine Principle. The mindset that *masculine* equals *male* might be too firmly established and the fear of changing it too strong. Or, like adults learning a foreign language, they will always have a heavy "accent." The basic belief in relationship of The Feminine Principle model might be more easily transmitted to boys growing up under the care of women who recognize the power of the model to enrich the lives of their sons. These boys, along with their sisters, will become adults who speak and think fluently together in a new Principle of Wholeness.

Finally, what makes it clear that The Feminine Principle is a model is that many women have been able to master the masculine way of thinking. Women who came into the business community thirty-five years ago had no choice but to learn to think like men, so they did. In interviews I did for this book, women who learned to think like men were not necessarily threatened by the idea that they would become men. It is fascinating to note that there is no equivalent word for *emasculation* that applies to women.

Each year, many people—women and men—question my championing of The New Feminine Principle. They assume that only a woman can effectively present this information. This might be true if—and this is a very big "if"—all women were seen as first-class citizens. Unfortunately, often they are not.

When a woman says the way women think is our best starting point for a new, viable future, the culture at large ignores her. When a man says the very same thing, his voice has a better chance of penetrating the cultural mindset. There is power speaking about this as a man.

This "deaf ear" is also indicative of the changes in attitude that must occur to have the voice of women's leadership heard as the brilliant alternative it is to the kind of leadership that has us in war after war and is fast destroying our environment.

How to Read This Book

This is a how-to book focused on self-discovery that is not primarily written for an academic or scientific or business audience. It is written for people from all walks of life who want to live and lead in wholeness. It is written with the intention of your recognizing, not my proving. There is no pressure to believe anything. My advice is to take what is useful and discard the rest.

This book is, by and large, addressed to women, though I would be personally delighted if many men read it and used the material within. If you are a woman, you will recognize the material in this book on a powerful intuitive level.

I have spent more than twenty-seven years involved in the movement to end hunger and starvation worldwide in our lifetime.

It is one of my primary commitments. After nearly three decades of educating myself, I know two things for certain:

1. When people are chronically malnourished, their ability to grow and thrive physically is stunted.

2. When people are systematically deprived of the opportunity to express their genius, to speak about their visions, or take a stand for their greatness, their spirit is stunted and their potential is limited.

Because of this, nourishment is the "master key" to the other keys, particularly Capacity. Frankly, you cannot even begin to speak about The Feminine Principle without honoring the nurturance that is a primary aspect of this belief system. If you are a woman, the opportunity is to use The New Feminine Principle deliberately and consciously to nourish in yourself what has been systematically starved out of a thousand generations of women. To break the chain of that starvation in yourself might be the single most powerful act of leadership you can make. If you are a man, this will almost certainly be a brand-new world for you. Think of this model as relocating to France and learning to live the way the French people do. I also recommend that you use the material presented here to open up powerful conversations with the women in your life.

The ultimate aim of this book is to create a wave of effective new leadership based on the basic belief system of women and filled out with powers and privileges that are traditionally reserved for men, allowing anyone to use it consciously and powerfully. How you use that power is your unique contribution to leadership in our world.

As a reader, if you come away from this book with the idea that what you call reality is only a series of beliefs, you will have gained an immense power to create as you go. If you follow some of the guidelines in this book, you will unleash that power in the direction of more freedom and effectiveness for you and the people around you.

Last of all, a secret! Though this is a serious subject, the best thing you can do to learn the material is to have some fun with it. There is no right answer to get. Do the experiments that appeal to you. Use the smorgasbord approach: take what you like and leave the rest.

It is undeniable that the clock of our final chapter as a species is ticking loudly, and that if left unchecked, the havoc that we have created worldwide will inevitably kill us all. It is also certain that in the bodies and souls of more than three billion women and girls and the men who champion them lies the genius, the spirit of our wholeness and sanity that can be expressed in a coherent model that gives everyone power. This spirit, which has always expressed itself in the privacy of family life, is now finally demanding to be expressed in the world at large.

As such, it is an amazing and miraculous time to be alive.

Acknowledgments

To Marie Butler-Knight, my publisher and editor, I would like to express my deep thanks for recognizing the material in this book as something of value to women and for her ability to organize the material so that it made the most sense.

To my agent, Judy Frank, I would like to express my gratitude for her commitment to have my work in the world at large and for standing by my side as I go out into the larger public.

To Mary Keil, who, more than anyone else in these last several years, has been my partner in launching the ideas in this book into the world and who has stood unyieldingly for the value of this work, I am deeply indebted.

My thanks to Lauri and Charles Kibby and Lynda Paulson and Hunter Quistgard, who have provided family roots in Southern California.

There have been so many people who have championed this work, without whose love, encouragement, and personal contribution none of this would be possible. And so, my thanks to Ellen Nash, Val Cook Watkins, Carole Alexander, Deborah Kelley, Reverend Goddess Sofreeyah, Reverend Barbara Thomas-Smith, Mary Elizabeth Young and Bob Bolender, Sarah Harper Lansburgh, Diane Covington, Fay Freed and Jewel Baldwin, Loma Alexander, Burke Franklin, Andrea Martin, Richard Gellernter, Peggy Francis, and Reesa Manning.

Finally, I would like to deeply acknowledge Joan Holmes and the people of The Hunger Project who have taught me to think new futures and have shown me how to do it in ways that have grown and fed me.

Trademarks

Chapter 1

When Systems Fail

If you are like most people, you have or love children. You want them to live in a world that is viable and safe. You want a life for them with a real chance for happiness.

This beautiful world we live in is a mess. The best guess is that our grandchildren will live to see the end of the human race if we continue the way we are going. About one fourth of our oceans are already polluted. Forests, which provide oxygen and help prevent our world from becoming a desert, are being destroyed at an almost unimaginably rapid rate. Our savage abuse of animal life is causing an unbridled extinction of irreplaceable living treasures. The faster the destruction, the more frenzied we seem to get.

One billion people go to bed hungry every night. Most of them are women and children. Globally, women earn less, are fed less, have less access to health care and education than men, and are brutalized, subjugated, and exploited by men in ways that most people cannot even begin to come to grips with. The rest of us are fed a physical diet that is loaded with hundreds of artificial ingredients that our biology simply has no way to handle and an intellectual diet that more and more resembles fast food for the soul. Tension over the possibility—and the actuality—of war is constant. Only the participants change. The rhetoric remains the same.

None of these conditions began recently. We are simply watching the snowball effect on phenomena that have been rolling downhill—some for millennia—and now have gathered frightening momentum.

The explanations that we are given to account for the mess we are in have no power. Some explanations are simply attempts to cast blame—on our educational or religious systems, political leaders, or economic policies. Other explanations justify and reinforce the idea that human beings get what they deserve because somehow we are a flawed species. A common explanation is that we are living for a next, better life, rather than this one. Overwhelmed by a morass of explanations that have no real power to change things, many people just want to get their piece of the pie and ignore the rest.

We are nearing a time of final deadlock. Clearly, the road we are on is a dead end. Though we pray that science will save us, science is only as good as the scientists who practice it, and they are trapped in the same quandary as the rest of us.

The Breakdown of The Masculine Principle

It is easy to blame men—or more popularly, testosterone—for the problems that plague us, while the real culprit goes unseen, ignored, or unexamined. That culprit is the systematic training of boys in a particularly harsh version of The Masculine Principle, called the dominator model. Dr. Riane Eisler, in her groundbreaking work *The Chalice and the Blade*, describes the dominator model as the culture of ruthless domination, especially directed at women. This "cult" of masculinity is epitomized in its extreme by Stalin, Hitler, Idi Amin, and political, social, and religious fundamentalists of all persuasions. Now it has also targeted the very ecosystem we live in and the genetic processes of people, animals, and plants as something to dominate and control. It is a cult that worships extreme competition and violence as the hallmarks of real masculinity and glorifies war as man's ultimate and most glorious "sport."

The language of the dominator model has penetrated every aspect of our lives. The "war" on terrorism, poverty, and drugs; the "fight against" cancer, heart disease, injustice, and hundreds of other things; even the "battle" of the sexes—these slogans suggest that to live is to be at war. Fight, fight, and fight. It might help if we were winning, but the fighting goes on and on and on, with victory nowhere in sight.

The reason you cannot expect men to create the world changes that will allow us to be viable and sustainable as a human species is that men have no real training in relationship or coming to consensus. These qualities are not part of The Masculine Principle we teach our boys, and so are invisible to men. When push comes to shove, as it usually does in the world of boys on the playground or men in politics, the automatic solution is "hit back." In a press conference at the end of peace talks between Israel and Palestine held at Camp David, President Clinton said that if there had been any women present at those meetings, some agreement would have been achieved. Clearly, men alone were not able to accomplish harmony. All they could do was fight.

At the bottom of the dominator model, which Dr. Eisler estimates started several thousand years ago with the rise of Indo-European culture, is a last-man-standing mentality that values winning at any cost and identifies everyone else as the "loser." About twenty years ago, a male television announcer covering the Olympic Games asked a silver medalist how he felt being a loser. Unexpectedly, this blatant dominator-model remark caused such a firestorm of protest around the world that the announcer lost his job.

Finally, despite the material possessions that define us, we "haves" in the developed world are starved for quality of life, driven by the highly pressurized pace that we feel forced to maintain just to keep up with what we think we must have to feel good about ourselves. Many of us are living vicariously through a small, select group who appear to participate in the excitement of life, buying into the lie that celebrities of all kinds have lives that are more important or valuable, and certainly more exciting, than our own. Reality TV is mistaken for reality itself.

If the amount of terror pumped into us by the media were poison being pumped into our water supply, we would all be dead by now. Privacy is at an end. The degradation of our humanity in favor of sensationalism, especially graphic violence of all kinds, has permeated every aspect of our lives and we are losing our ability to respond. Though there really is plenty of it around, goodness gets little press. Good people persevere with little or no credit or attention, and people who represent the lower limit of the human experience get major airtime and front-page coverage.

The look of chronic tension and unhappiness on the faces of normal people on the street is appalling. Real courtesy seems to be a lost art. In major cities, we barely even acknowledge one another's existence, preferring to talk on our cell phones while we walk or put on headphones to listen to music. As the world has sped up externally, we have also sped up internally to the point where even short delays or small mistakes become triggers for emotional blowups that are completely out of proportion to the event.

As Albert Einstein advised, "The significant problems we face cannot be solved at the same level of thinking we had when we created them." We need to get it through our heads that something entirely new is called for!

The Wave of the Future

Though the current report is grim, take heart. There is a powerful wave of desire arising for a way to live and have the results we want in harmony with our deepest desire for happiness and in consideration of the billions of others with whom we share our world. It is a call for new leadership—not just different leaders, but a kind of leadership that has real potential to open doorways and make things new.

Women Are the Key

Is this new way to lead a breakthrough in technology? A new spiritual or esoteric insight? A revolutionary political system?

Hardly. The answer to the problems we face, though repeatedly overlooked or ignored, lives right in our own backyard. Where? It lives in women who have developed and passed on to their daughters, over the millennia, strategies to raise families and to organize powerfully and effectively the villages, neighborhoods, churches, community organizations, and social groups in which they live. It lives in the elements of their strategies that include results and a style of producing them that is inclusive and nourishing of everyone involved.

Though it is hard to believe, it was not until 1993 that the World Conference on Human Rights ratified the United Nations Universal Declaration of Human Rights, declaring at long last that women's rights are human rights. That such a proclamation would be necessary, let alone newsworthy, underscores the need for a new way of thinking and leading.

A close friend of mine attended the Beijing Women's Conference in 1995, where then-First Lady Hillary Clinton delivered the keynote address. In it she declared emphatically that "human rights are women's rights and women's rights are human rights." My friend recalled, "Before the meeting we were holding our breath, wondering if Mrs. Clinton would have the guts to make her statement about human rights. When Mrs. Clinton made her statement on women's rights, the meeting, which was thronged with thousands and thousands of women leaders from all around the world and thousands more standing outside in the rain, erupted in joy and happiness."

You could say that in the consciousness of the world at large, women are just on the sociological brink of becoming adults. Though shocking to consider, this fact enables us to focus on the unconsciousness with which we have treated (to use the words of the United Nations) our most valuable and underused resource. It also puts us on notice that, like a teenager entering puberty, women are beginning a "growth spurt," and everything about them is going to change dramatically. In this universal coming of age for women, there is hope for a real change, not just a rehash of everything we've already been doing.

Women have always been charged with bringing in new life and sustaining it. Women are imbued with a model of reality that focuses on the viability and growth of human beings. Who better to speak for the world we desire? Women are natural multitaskers. Over thousands of years, their need to keep track of many children simultaneously has developed their ability to think globally, i.e., take into account and synthesize many elements at the same time. Who better to get the whole picture regarding any issue of importance to humanity? Representing the heart of their families, women live in an intuitive realm that, although informed by intellect, is not subjugated by it. Who better to create the nonlinear leaps that will effectuate new ways of looking at global concerns and bring about original ways to deal with them?

Let's face it. To make a proclamation about the vital role of woman is one thing; however, to implement the changes in tradition and culture in a world dominated by a masculine view of "life as war, last man standing" is quite another.

The Stirrings of Power

In the United States and other developed countries, the modern Women's Movement has been a powerful force to be reckoned with for the last forty years. Its earliest efforts, though useful in that they called into question the whole masculine/feminine paradigm in which we think, were essentially resistive and combative; they were done in a style that mimicked the tactics of the very men who were seen as the agents of women's oppression. That tactical style created a deep schism in the Women's Movement itself, where to be feminist was to be "militant." This is a designation that most women see as the antithesis of what women have always stood for.

Perhaps the single most important outcome of the Women's Movement was the permission and encouragement that women gave one another to stop defining themselves solely as a reflection of their relationship with men.

We might laugh now, but thirty years ago, women in business wore dark suits that made them look like junior men because they "knew" that business is a man's game, played by men's rules. These rules were based on military models, with business as war, competition to beat, victories to be won, and heroism to be gained. These pioneering businesswomen tried to think and act like men because there was no other model. More pointedly, there was no validation of the model that they themselves used. Being second-class people in a male-dominated world, their way of doing things was also considered second-class. If you were a woman, you were forced to try to beat men at their own game— often using the same worn-out, aggressive strategies that kill men early. Being the brilliant and flexible people they are, many women learned to play and win this man's game, though often with the same consequent problems and debilities that have befallen men.

Claiming the Future

Times have certainly changed. With the end of the manufacturing age and the inauguration and acceleration of the information age, the emphasis on muscle power has shifted to an emphasis on brainpower. The playing field is being leveled in ways that would have been impossible to imagine even a few years ago.

Women are coming into corporate power at every level. They are the fastest-growing population of small business owners in the United States and are reinventing the style in which business is conducted. These small business owners have the freedom to decide for themselves how they will conduct their businesses.

When women realized that they have the power to choose, they went beyond the bottom line and began to include all the elements that are important to them. Intangibles like work environment, opportunity for networking and friendship, cooperation and inclusivity, the well-being of their families, spirituality, even fun became essential elements of their personal and business strategies. Moreover, most women have no interest in working in the driven style that they see detracts from the quality of life men have. As elsewhere in life for women, results and style became equally important in the workplace. At first defensive, men have sat up and taken notice and begun to rethink their own rehashed military strategies.

In a speech given by President Nelson Mandela, this heroic man said that when Black people were freed from apartheid in South Africa, the White people of South Africa were freed as well. Mr. Mandela said that as long as apartheid existed, Whites and Blacks were both imprisoned and victimized by the system. When the "prison" crumbled, both the jailers and the prisoners were free to go on with their lives. Similarly, as women have freed themselves from the delusion that they have to play the game of business or public life the way men have traditionally played it, they have also freed men to rethink their priorities, their work styles, and what they expect from their lives. This is real leadership in action.

The feminine style of getting things done, thousands of years old, presents a unique opportunity to produce extraordinary results in a brand-new way in every area of human endeavor, not just in families where it has been road tested most extensively. In the United States, where the culture of business is evolving exponentially, this style is the wave of the future. As people realize that the idea of (paternalistic) corporations taking care of them for the rest of their lives is a thing of the past, they recognize the need for a whole new way of thinking and getting things done. One thing is easily recognizable: this is a time when the ability to invent is the winning hand.

In a speech I attended recently, Dr. Wendy Flint of the Training and Development Center of the College of the Desert told us that $100 billion (yes, billion) is being spent every year for training and development by companies in North America. Of that staggering amount, the vast bulk is being spent to inculcate what have traditionally been called "soft skills"—effective communication, the ability to relate and work in teams, and customer service. Dr. Flint said that the Human Resources manager of a major international software company told her in no uncertain terms that unless engineers (a traditional masculine role) had these people skills (traditional feminine qualities), he just was not interested in hiring them.

Dr. Flint attributed this change in attitude to the change in the business environment, which has undergone a radical shift from industrial production to information production. In an age of information, she emphasized, sales and service are the most important business activities, not physical products themselves. Every person—woman and man—needs to adjust, but women have a clear edge over men in the world we have entered.

The feminine style is the basis for the wave of the future, not just for women, but for everyone who intends to be successful in the information age. To have power with this style it is urgent for women and men to realize that The Feminine Principle is a model, a view of reality—not reality itself—that can be used by anyone and can be changed when you are aware of its beliefs and mechanics. To lead in The Feminine Principle is not just to discover how it lives in you, but also to discover how to modify and customize it to meet the requirements of your own life. In the world of information, The New Feminine Principle is the jackpot.

Chapter 2

Models Invent Reality

At the heart of the dilemmas we face as individuals and as a world is a fact whose power goes largely unchallenged. Even the most educated people fail to grasp this simple, central fact: the systems of thinking and behavior we live in are simply models of reality, a shared view of what is occurring at any given moment. A model, plainly stated, is a system of belief that someone invents to explain, predict, and control (or create a feeling of control over) phenomena that are occurring, and to which others consent or agree—sometimes just a few, sometimes millions or billions.

Turn off your analytical mind and feel the emotional impact of this piece of information: someone made up your religious, political, economic, medical, scientific, and cultural systems. The way you gesture, the language you use, how you eat, what you eat, your social class, what success or failure look like, and the very way you think were all made up long before you were ever born.

You did not invent any of these things you take for granted. You simply inherited them. You are also not stuck with them. The models we use now are not necessarily the way it has to be; they are just what other people have invented that you, by your cooperation with their invention, affirm.

Real but Not True

Models are not necessarily "true," i.e., absolute; however, they gain an enormous power of reality by the belief that you, intentionally or unintentionally, invest in them. Ironically, when you invest a model with your belief, it becomes real or true *for you*.

Your experiences validate your system of belief, because you are looking for and interpreting phenomena in favor of it.

Imagine you lived ten thousand years ago. Natural phenomena were powerful, frightening, and often capricious. In order to assert control—or at least the illusion of control—over these phenomena, you and the people of your tribe began to attribute them to vast, giant beings, gods if you will, who controlled the weather and therefore your future. You began to imagine what these gods would accept as offerings to win them to your side or at least to placate them so they would not harm you. You created ceremonies, made material offerings, and developed a set of rules by which you lived in order to interact with these fearsome beings. To your delight, these ceremonies, offerings, and rules worked! For many years, the weather patterns in your area remained mild and benevolent. Your explanation of reality and your ability to control it were obviously "true."

One day, a sudden, terrifying event occurred. The very earth you stood on began to shake so violently that everyone and everything were thrown to the ground. The earth opened and swallowed half of your tribe. In a few moments, everything you knew and valued was destroyed. After the disaster, you met with other survivors from your tribe and discovered that you had been living on a major fault line.

No, strike that. The model that created fault-line theory was not invented yet. You decided that the gods who controlled your physical environment must be furious with something that your tribe had done or had forgotten to do. You decided that new, more stringent ceremonies and practices must be established in order to placate the gods and that a whole new level of material offerings was in order. Human life, clearly the most important material gift you had, began to be sacrificed. For many years thereafter, the earth was quiet. Your belief in fearsome gods and your own attempts to placate them were validated and made you powerful in the face of the unpredictable.

If you had been born in the fifteenth century, you would have believed absolutely that the sun revolved around the earth because Aristotle, the ancient "last word" on all things intellectual, thought it did. When Copernicus found evidence that the earth traveled around the sun, he created a controversy that lasted nearly two hundred years. So powerful was this belief that the astronomer Galileo was silenced by the Church for his adamant support of Copernicus's view. Once a belief is deeply imbedded in the cultural consciousness, it gains a power of its own that can be difficult to counteract.

Did you know that when automobiles were first introduced to the public, a model of physical endurance strongly held by physicians and scientists asserted that if automobiles traveled at more than 60 mph, human beings would die from the stress on their bodies? Did you also know that less than one hundred years ago, our models of medicine and physiology were absolutely certain that the physical stress of athletic competition would be dangerous for most women? Did you know that, less than fifty years ago, the quadruple jump in Olympic ice-skating was considered impossible?

Models Create Our Reality

Consider this: you live in models of reality at this very moment that go largely unexamined and that you validate by fitting into them, even if they limit your capacity for leadership, greatness, or even happiness. At the core of what it is to be a woman or a man is a set of beliefs that silences women and cuts the hearts out of men. No wonder there is a battle of the sexes.

Unless you have the great gift and privilege of being a truly original thinker, the models you use basically live your life for you. In a manner of speaking, they invent you, by telling you how you should be, what you should think, and how you should act. They talk to you in your head, like public-service announcements for your belief systems. Many people have thousands of thoughts per hour without any ability to turn them off. Belief systems you hold can even be diametrically opposed to one another, creating the feeling that you are at war with yourself about certain areas of your life.

These models are like automatic default settings in you, unless you consciously enlarge, reinvent, or replace them. Rebellion does not help, as you have probably discovered by now. You have to put yourself on "manual" and consciously reprogram the settings. Some complex home entertainment systems have a default setting when you turn them on—the CD player, the television, the FM receiver. No matter what you were using when you turned off the system, the default setting is automatically activated when you turn your entertainment system back on. It's the same with your own default settings. For example, no matter how much you tell yourself in a meeting that you will speak up this time, you might find yourself going to your "default setting" of pretending you have nothing to say. To lead, you have to get beyond the default settings. Life in leadership is life on manual.

The consensual belief of millions of people who came before you endows models with an immense power to create reality. Your parents, church, and social groups teach you the models they believe in and tell you, "That's life (reality)." Sometimes you like what you get from their models; sometimes you don't.

We are rarely taught that models are simply our best attempt to explain things that happen, because our parents and other authority figures themselves are under the hypnotic spell of the models that are using them. Our underlying assumption is that the realities generated by the models we live in are just the way it is. People who live that way when times change are often called traditionalists, conservatives, or simply "old fossils."

Change the Model and You Change Reality

After you know that it might be the model you live in that is the real problem, why stay in it? There are three compelling reasons.

1. Most people do not have the skills necessary to examine the models in which they live and to change them.
2. Though many people, after they discover the idea of models, would like to abandon a model they are using, they have no viable alternative, so they continue to try harder and harder to make the one they have work.
3. Like the cartoon character who runs off the cliff and stays in midair until she realizes where she is, the very idea that you have nothing to stand on but your beliefs is anxiety provoking, to say the least.

When I discovered the truth about models, I felt ice in the pit of my stomach and a feeling of anxiety, as if something were warning me away from this information because it was dangerous. Powerful emotions and strong sensations surround the programming we get about reality. We learn it early, and it is well protected. Alarm bells go off as we get closer to the edge of belief. This explains why people often feel freaked out when they are faced with brand-new information or experiences. It also explains why some people refuse to change at all.

From time to time, people have a sudden epiphany so strong and undeniable that it takes them out beyond these alarms, and they find themselves in a brand-new world. We call these people visionaries, geniuses, saints, or madwomen, depending on our point of view. Consider Joan of Arc: she heard voices that directed her to save France from the British, was burnt at the stake as a witch for hearing those same voices, and after death was speedily "rehabilitated" in reputation and became a saint of the Catholic Church. Nothing about her actual life changed, only the system of belief from which she was seen.

Models are best guesses about what is really going on, how often it will occur, and ultimately what to do about it or how to use it. They are systems that organize perception, grant coherence, and are, in turn, validated by "evidence." They are most often closed, self-validating systems that ignore or attack any evidence to the contrary.

Models are the basis for self-fulfilling prophecies, because people always look for evidence to validate their models of belief. Did you know that subatomic particles have been shown to respond to the predictions made about them by the people who are observing and working with them? What does that say about so-called reality, independent of our belief?

When Models Are the Problem

Religious and social models invent good and bad, right and wrong, socially acceptable or not, and scores of rules to live by. This is not inherently bad. It is simply the nature of models.

You did not invent what it is to be feminine or masculine. You did not invent your culture, your language, your religion, or your social standards. They were here generations before you ever showed up. You didn't even choose them. You "grew up" with them, meaning that they were transmitted to you without your conscious choice from the day you were born. You did not even invent your name; it was given to you.

Models give coherence to life. They are valuable because they are useful. A model can give you more ability to predict and interpret events and act purposefully to have more of what you desire. This gives rise to the question: what do human beings desire? What is the fundamental human desire? Across cultures, people want viability for themselves, happiness for their children, and the continuation of life. Your parents wanted that for you; their parents wanted it for them. It's as simple as that. If you remember any time when you held a newborn, you will notice that it was completely natural to want the best for that child and to want her life to go on.

If the answer to the question of what people want is viability, happiness, and continuity, the real question is: why would we *not* use a model of reality that generates and focuses on happiness up front? That model is The New Feminine Principle, which we will examine closely in Chapter 3.

Models are not writ in stone; they are writ in thought, both conscious and unconscious. If a model stops giving you more of what you want, the model becomes a problem. Like any system of thought, a model can be changed as new information is received, if you have access to the "architecture" of the model itself and know how to use it. To illustrate, let's use the example of the operating system that enables you to use your computer. It sets up the parameters of what you can and cannot do on your computer. When you know how to operate the computer system, you have one kind of power. When you know how the operating system is designed and can reprogram it, you have a whole different kind of power. Any model of reality that does not give you a full experience of happiness and sustainability can be changed at any moment. Regardless of what your parents, religion, social group, or peers think, you have the right to change any belief that does not contribute to your sense of real happiness and viability. First, you have to be conscious of what the model is and how it operates. That is the essence of leadership that hopes to achieve anything new.

Models vs. Experience

Models are not what you actually experience. They are the perceptual frameworks that allow you to interpret your experience. The way in which you understand something dictates how you feel about it, the actions you take, what you expect from the experience you are having, and ultimately your satisfaction or dissatisfaction. Quite literally, it's all what you make of it.

Let me give you an example. Your body temperature is 100.3°F and you feel fatigued. (These are just experiences. Inherently, they mean nothing in particular.) You go to an allopathic physician, someone trained in the Western medical model. She

explains (based on her system of belief) that you have a mild infec-
tion. She gives you an antibiotic and tells you it will kill the germs
that are attacking you. (Notice the way that the Western medical
system, which historically has been the exclusive enclave of men,
focuses on giving you back your health by fighting, a central male
tactic.) Or you go to an acupuncturist and she tells you (based on
her system of belief) that your body pulses are not in balance. She
gives you a treatment to balance your pulses and tells you that this
treatment will help to restore your energetic balance and therefore
your health. Or you go to your grandmother. She also has her own
system of belief. She says you are working too hard and prescribes
a vacation. She also gives you a hot toddy with a large shot of whis-
key, tells you how much she loves you, and gives you a casserole to
take home, because "You wouldn't get sick if you were eating more
home-cooked food."

Herbalist, physician, faith healer, nutritionist, medical intuitive,
chiropractor, shaman, grandmother—all of them view the same
experience, but from entirely different models. Consider a visit to
the Empire State Building in New York. You and your mate take
the elevator to the observatory and split up to look around. You
stand on the north side and see Central Park. Your mate stands on
the south side and sees the Statue of Liberty in the harbor. Though
you are both in the observatory of the very same building, you have
completely different views of New York City. In other words, *where
you are standing when you view something* is the main determiner of
what you see and of the power you have to act on what you have
seen. Models are just like that.

The "Try Harder" Fallacy

Unfortunately, even when the prescriptions of the models in which
you live do not help, if you are like most people, you will validate
the model you live in, presume it is you who are wrong, and try
harder. Our culture particularly is a try-harder culture, and people
run themselves into the ground redoubling their efforts till there is

nothing left. Traditions, training, and cultural conditioning can be hard to break, as we know from people who continue to spend holidays with their families doing things they have never enjoyed, hoping that somehow this year it will be different.

Several years ago, I interviewed a woman who had worked for an advertising agency. She told me that the owner of the agency was a man who lived in the military model and used analogies like "taking the hill" for meeting a goal. For several years his agency, which opened during a boom time, had all the work it could handle and his main concern was hiring enough people to meet the workload. When the economy cooled and less work came in, he called an "emergency" meeting, laid off two or three employees, and asked his remaining staff to work an hour extra every day to make up for the employees who had been laid off. "Each week," she said, "we had another meeting to discuss the 'crisis' at the agency. And each week we were asked to take on more responsibility and work longer hours. Finally, when we were asked to work seven days a week, ten hours a day, I quit. My boss actually called me a sellout. But I know in my heart if my boss had included in our planning the fluctuations that are normal for our business, there wouldn't have been an 'emergency' at all. Trying harder was no solution. The solution was to look at the business in a completely different way."

More importantly, if something you want is not a part of the model you are using, you simply have no access to it. Recently I read a short biography of Edith Wharton, a brilliant writer born in 1862 who won the Pulitzer Prize for her insightful novels about the traps and foibles of the New York upper class, of which she was a member. She said that in her social class women were not expected to write anything except social notes to one another. They were certainly not expected to be well educated, have a mind of their own, or have anything original to say. When Edith felt the desire to write stories as a child, she knew she could not ask her mother for paper. It was unthinkable that a girl of class

would want to be a writer and she knew her mother would immediately say no. Many girls gave up their own personal dreams
to the demands of being young ladies in their families' model of
social class. Edith's desire, however, was so powerful that she "invented" writing paper of her own by saving the wrappings from
packages that came to her home and writing stories on them.

Inventing a New Model

Your mindset, which remains, for the most part, invisible and unexamined, is the profound background against which your life is
shaped and played out. To examine your cultural "legacy" and
change it from the inside out is one form of leadership genius.

In the 1960s, the Black Panthers realized that a social model
that validated white people first had poisoned the spirit of black
people. In other words, just by being black, you were intrinsically "less than." No matter what you did, you would never be
white—and white was definitely "right." In a stroke of genius,
the Panthers created a new model by teaching African American
parents and children a simple and powerful idea: "Black is beautiful." This idea became a chant that, when absorbed by millions of
African Americans, changed their whole cultural point of view and
became a background against which everything showed up differently. It also changed the white American cultural point of view
along with it and swept us into a new era.

Real leadership might have more to do with examining and
changing the model you are using than handling conditions or
problems that are caused by the model. In medicine, physicians
are acutely aware that symptomatic relief is entirely different from
a cure.

If you can use the model but you cannot see the place from
which the model is generated, you are powerless to make any lasting change, because the default setting of the model will always
be in play. Most women, though competent with The Feminine
Principle (model), have not mastered it. They can use it but have

no power to change it, because to change it would require that they recognize that the feminine style comes from a model of reality, not from their gender. When you can consciously see how the model is formulated and distinguish it from the culture of subjugation that has plagued our species, you have real power to make permanent changes. Consider that consciously examining the models of reality in which you live is like Toto pulling back the curtain and exposing the ordinary man who was operating the machinery that made the Wizard of Oz seem so terrifyingly real and powerful.

One of the central aims of this book is to give you the power to use The Feminine Principle consciously, distinguishing it from the cultural interpretation that has grown up around it.

Models of Gender: Feminine and Masculine

The Feminine Principle, like all models of belief, starts from a central assertion, a seed from which the entire system sprouts and grows. The assertion of The Feminine Principle is that *life is connected and holographic*; that is, everything and everyone is essentially related, and everything and everyone is a microcosm of life at large (more on this in Chapter 3). When you begin with the idea that everything is already connected, you create an environment where relatedness is the essential medium in which you live, not unlike water being the essential medium in which fish live and by which each and every thing that lives in the ocean is joined. The idea that everything and everyone is a microcosm of life at large gives us a commonality with other human beings and species that makes ecology make sense. Did you know that more than 99 percent of the genetic makeup of all human beings is identical? The prejudices we hold about other races and ethnicities, even gender, clearly comes from our learned models rather than anything intrinsic.

Truthfully, as a man I have thought long and hard about what the primary assertion of The Masculine Principle is that gives rise to the condition of individuality, a focus on personal power and competition, and an emphasis on freedom and results at any cost. After nearly fifteen years of this inquiry, I can honestly say that the way I have come to understand the primary assertion of The Masculine Principle is that *nothing is essentially related or holographic*; that is, everyone and everything stands on his own, and one thing (person) is not essentially like another. When you begin with the idea that nothing is essentially related, you create an environment where individuality is the medium in which you live. Unfortunately, the experience of this individuality is often a feeling of isolation, aloneness, or me-against-the world, the existential crisis of modern human beings, especially men.

The difference in these assertions is clearly evidenced by the behavior of women and men in every part of the world. Women are normally more social; men, more solitary. Women value inclusion; men value personal freedom. In the developing world, men in villages who earn money often buy cigarettes, alcohol, and radios first, while women in the same villages who earn money buy food and other essentials first and share them with other women and children in the village. In our own developed world, the Center for Women's Business Research reports that "Women entrepreneurs describe their businesses in family terms and see their business relationships as a network. Men entrepreneurs think in hierarchical terms and focus more on establishing clear rules and procedures." These examples shed a powerful light on the models within which women and men think and how the models they use affect their personal decisions to behave in particular ways.

As a man, I have had to come to grips with the whole idea that what we call "being a man" might be based on a single misconception or negation of what seems to be the way life everywhere operates. In the physical sciences, the theories of relativity, unified field, and particles physics all point to the same thing, namely, that everything and everyone everywhere are in relationship with one another.

In a corporate training I facilitated, a vice president argued that no one had really given him anything and that he had achieved success all by himself—a real boot-strap type. I asked him to do an experiment, and reluctantly, he agreed. I pointed out that the expensive suit and watch he was wearing, the chair he was sitting on, the food he had for breakfast, and the car in which he had driven to the meeting were all given to him through the cooperation of millions of people. He agreed, but said it was his money that allowed him to buy the things I mentioned. I pointed out that the money and credit he used were the invention of others, as were his language, education, and the culture in which he lived. His name, even his own body were the creations of other people. His basic survival as a child was the gift of others. I asked him to take in this information, which he agreed was true, and then see how it fit his model of success on his own. First he frowned and said nothing. Then after a minute or two, he started to laugh and said uncharacteristically, "You mean I'm not the only one living on this planet?" The entire tone and result of the meeting changed from that point on. We were still sitting in chairs in an office building, having a meeting about his team's performance. What changed was the model that this man was using, the place from which he was viewing his experience. A new starting point gave him a completely different world to live in.

A Startling Revelation

Nowhere in the central primary assertions of The Feminine or Masculine Principles is there any actual reference to gender. It is vitally important to realize that The Feminine Principle and the feminine style are not necessarily functions of female biology any more than the way men operate is fundamentally derived from the biological fact of their maleness.

Frankly, the quality and variety of choices that human beings enjoy transcend the boundaries of biological determinism, including gender. For example, like animals, human beings need to eat, but the styles of eating and the rituals of eating that human beings engage in are quantum leaps from anything else in the animal kingdom. Too, women are the only females in the animal world who have complete freedom to choose their sexual behavior outside of the dictates of estrus. At the extreme, transsexuals report being one gender trapped in the body of the other gender. Clearly, gender itself is not the source of our image of who we are. Our ability to create cultural structures, mores, and expressions puts us in a league of our own.

The sum total of human civilization can easily be seen as the on-going endeavor to transcend our inheritance from the animal kingdom and become something more, motivated by drives other than survival alone. Viewed through this lens, the dominator model is exposed for what it might really be, an outmoded expression of our animal inheritance that is no longer desirable or even useful.

The Problem of Mastery

A startling truth that I have discovered is that although women are "native speakers" of The Feminine Principle, they do not necessarily have conscious mastery of it. Most women live in the feminine style the way most men live in the masculine style, i.e., never questioning it, observing only the effect of the style, and rarely making the distinctions that would give them the power to alter it.

Most women live as if the feminine style is just the way it is for women. Men do the same with the masculine style. The reason for this is that most women and men were not given the opportunity to choose freely one style or the other so they never *consciously* chose to live in one style or the other. Their gender was the sole determinant of what they were taught to believe about themselves and the world around them.

The pitfalls women face in The Feminine Principle, as we currently transmit it to girls, are addiction to relationship and emotion, the need to talk everything out (sometimes over and over), the inability to wield power and make clear-cut decisions, and a sense of being second-class. The pitfalls men face in The Masculine Principle, as we currently transmit it to boys, are devaluing emotion, going it alone, and a propensity for incessant competition and domination. What is clear is that both genders are limited in their ability to speak about aspects of their experience that do not fall easily or readily into their gender-based reality. What is also clear is that both genders know instinctively that something is missing from their view of the world.

In Chapter 3, I'll look more closely at the positive and negative aspects of The Feminine Principle. For now, it's only important to remember that any set of beliefs can be changed anytime it proves to be inadequate for giving you the results you desire. There is nothing writ in stone about the way women and men think. It is only and always written in belief.

Models of Leadership

For many human beings, leadership resides in the leader herself, not in a model of leadership. This is the same kind of confusion that surrounds The Feminine and Masculine Principles when you view them as functions of biology rather than models of belief. When you know that leadership really resides in a model rather than in a person, you gain the power to master the model and become a leader in your own right. More important, once you learn how the model operates, you gain the power to change it any way you like—even to invent a new model of leadership, if you choose.

Aside from models of leadership themselves, there are literally hundreds of permutations and combinations of *styles* that leaders have used over the millennia, based on their own unique personalities. It is certainly easy to confuse the style with the model; however, when you extract the personality style of the leader and look at the model she is using, you see that there may be only four basic models of leadership: control, pioneering, demonstration, and empowerment. It is crucial to keep reminding yourself that models are not "true," but rather systems of belief that someone made up and others bought into.

Leadership by Control

In the world as we have known it, leadership typically comes from military might and reflects the particularly harsh version of The Masculine Principle called the dominator model. Leadership by control arises from The Masculine Principle and is the model of leadership with which we are most familiar. It is command based on hierarchy and the power to compel compliance under threat of punishment. It is the domination of the weaker by the stronger. This is practiced by nearly every country of the world, including the United States. At the far end of the continuum, absolute dictatorship, as practiced by the likes of "strongman" François "Papa Doc" Duvalier of Haiti, arises over and over in the dominator model. It represents the epitome of domination, often with crippling effects for the people of the countries in which such dictatorship is practiced.

In the military, women and men are taught to obey orders based on rank alone. To disobey an order results in punishments ranging from reprimand to death. Police forces, which are paramilitary organizations, follow this same type of leadership. Absolute monarchies, churches, oppressive leadership, top-down organizations of all kinds, and even schools, for the most part, operate under the aegis of hierarchy and power to compel compliance under threat of punishment. The vast majority of our legal system is based on this model.

Even though actual punishment might be seldom used, the threat of punishment compels compliance through the experience of fear. For most people driving down a highway, the sight of a police car pulling up behind them will inspire instant fear that they will be punished, even if they are doing nothing illegal or if the police are not interested in them. This is a model where people are less complying with the law than avoiding the risk of feeling or looking guilty. This is also a model that completely ignores the behavioral data that punishment works to suppress behavior for a time but does not eliminate it. The speeding ticket that kept you within the speed limit for a week has no power to compel you to do so in a month or two.

The truism of this kind of leadership is "Only the strong survive."

Leadership by Pioneering

Leadership by pioneering is outside the dominator model. It goes where no one has gone before and leaves a trail that others can follow. People who pioneer may or may not do so with any conscious intention for leadership or control. People who set out for new lands, make new inventions, or experiment with new ways to live or think are pioneers.

Though you might not realize it, if you are a woman who has started her own business, you are pioneering a whole new business frontier. Women are the fastest growing segment of new businesses in the United States. You are part of a phenomenon that is changing the face of American business. As a woman, your style is creating the wave of the future for people who work in the information age.

Do you think about being a pioneer? Do you realize you are leading the way for women around the world? Are you aware that as a middle-class American woman you have education, freedom, and power that almost no women in the history of the world have had? Probably not. More likely you think about doing something you are good at, making the kind of money you want, and providing for yourself and your family.

Pioneering is invisible to you on the day-to-day level. Consider that in the history of the world at large, you are a woman who, just by being who you are and living the life you do, is shattering images and ideas about women that have persisted for many thousands of years.

On the other hand, there are women in India who are consciously pioneering a brand-new way of government. When the Indian government passed a law that all the village councils in India had to be made up of at least 30 percent women, a new world opened. Women who had never been out of their villages ran for office, were elected, and became leaders for the first time in the history of their country. They are thoroughly aware that they represent an historic opportunity for women to have a voice in the future of their villages and India itself. This way of leading is called a pioneering effort, because the intention of a group of committed individuals consciously altered the model of reality in which they lived.

The truism of this kind of leadership is (to paraphrase *Star Trek*) "To boldly go where no one has gone before."

Leadership by Demonstration

Leadership by demonstration, also outside the dominator model, is the ability to embody in your speaking, actions, and results the principles to which you adhere. This is a much higher level of leadership than control or pioneering because it requires an internal integrity that is not much practiced these days. Within this model of leadership, you would not ask anyone to do anything that you had not done yourself. It also requires a conscious attention to the details of the way you speak and how you achieve results—external as well as internal integrity.

Consider in your own life people you have known who really "walk their talk." They may or may not do it consciously. They may or may not do it to inspire others. Conscious of their inspiration or not, they wield the power to make us want to be like them. They are our role models, our inspiration, because who they are on the inside is lined up with who they present themselves as being on the outside.

If you had asked me almost anytime in my adult life, I would have said that I am committed to peace. What I wouldn't have told you is that I wasn't peaceful inside. You probably would have noticed it anyway.

About eleven years ago, I had a startling realization. I began to listen to the language I used and realized that in my everyday language, I was projecting violence and killing nearly every single time I opened my mouth. I wanted a "killer" look when I dressed. I described certain foods as "to die for." I wanted my favorite team to "massacre" its opponents.

On an impulse, I made a list of common expressions that the media or my friends or I used to describe violently events that were essentially nonviolent. I filled up seven pages of single-spaced, loose-leaf paper in less than ten minutes. I was astounded. Over the next few months, I worked to delete these phrases from my vocabulary. I discovered that I had holes in my language where I couldn't think of another way to say what I wanted to say without violence. Over more than a year, I worked to construct a new vocabulary of phrases, with two surprising results:

1. My ability to communicate powerfully and colorfully went up so much that people started commenting on the brilliant way I used language.

2. The internal anxiety and turmoil I was experiencing dropped dramatically and I realized that they were the direct results of the internal dialogue I was having with myself to describe my world.

The truism of this kind of leadership, in Mahatma Gandhi's words, is "We must be the change we wish to see."

Leadership by Empowerment

Leadership by empowerment transcends the other three kinds of leadership to produce the power of real authority. This kind of leadership demands that you demonstrate competence to speak, act, and get results in your desired enterprise. It also requires that you pioneer new territory by inquiring more deeply into what is already known and held to be "true." With the freedom to question and inquire comes the power to make innovations

that push out the boundaries of knowledge and experience. It requires that you grow yourself into someone who inspires others
to follow your lead to realize your visions and goals. At its highest
level, this kind of leadership is known by its ability to help others
become leaders in their own right. This is true visionary leadership.

I had the privilege of coaching the late Andrea Martin, the
founder of The Breast Cancer Fund. Andrea, a trial lawyer schooled
in New Orleans, was brainy and charismatic. She could create relationship with anyone. Her powers of "working a crowd" were leg-
endary. About five feet tall, with a brilliant smile and a great sense
of style and adventure, Andrea worked as a fundraiser in Senator
Dianne Feinstein's election campaign, drove a Harley motorcycle—
complete with black leather riding outfit—and could dress with the
elegance of a real San Francisco lady. When she tired of law and
politics, Andrea opened a Southern barbecue restaurant that was a
hit from day one.

Having recently married a man who idolized her, Andrea fit the
profile of someone who had hit the jackpot over and over. Then
in 1989, at age 42, she received a diagnosis of breast cancer and
was told to put her affairs in order. A year and a half later, having
beaten the first cancer, she was told she had a tumor in her remaining breast. She triumphed over that one as well.

With a young daughter and a new husband, Andrea rethought
her whole life. "I knew it would not be more of the same for me.
When I thought about my law background, my time in politics, and
my skills as the owner of a successful restaurant, it became apparent
to me that I had everything I needed to start an organization that
could make an impact on this issue. And it was something I did not
want my own daughter and other girls her age to have to face," she
told me over lunch one day. "I never looked back." In 1992, Andrea
started The Breast Cancer Fund in her living room to "transform
the breast cancer epidemic from a private secret to a public health
priority." The organization grew to a national force with more than
70,000 supporters.

Before she died of a brain tumor in 2003, Andrea climbed several mountains around the world with other breast cancer survivors to raise the world's consciousness about this epidemic. An original thinker, she masterminded an ad campaign, "Obsessed with Breasts," which showed her own surgical scars superimposed on beautiful young models. The campaign was picked up by the media and shown around the world. Andrea was instrumental in having a breast cancer postage stamp inaugurated, which has generated millions of dollars for breast cancer research. Leaving no stone unturned, one of Andrea's final acts was to travel to New York and Washington, D.C., to spotlight the role that environmental pollutants play in breast cancer. Millions saw her picture in a *New York Times* ad with the caption "Warning—Andrea Martin contains 59 cancer-causing industrial chemicals."

The integrity between what she said and did and the results she produced was Andrea's calling card. She pioneered a new way to view breast cancer and its causes, and she took every opportunity to lead the medical and political communities out of their entrenched ideas about breast cancer. She had a loyal following of people who were literally willing to do whatever she asked, because she demonstrated her own personal leadership every step of the way. Her legacy is that she empowered thousands of people around her to take their own stand for the end of breast cancer and to define for themselves what leadership would look like in their own lives. In other words, she "re-created" her spirit in the souls and hearts of the people around her so they could become leaders in their own right. When Andrea died, her close friend, Jeanne Rizzo, who had been inspired by Andrea's spirit and her work, took over the reins of The Breast Cancer Fund, which continues to represent the cutting edge of work to end breast cancer once and for all.

The truism of this kind of leadership is "Be fruitful and multiply."

Competence

In coaching, the term "unconscious competent" is used to describe people who naturally play well, but do not have distinctions that would give them mastery of their game. In order to become consciously competent, it is necessary to take yourself off "automatic pilot" and to examine what has, up to now, felt natural. For a time, you might even feel awkward and have the experience that your competence is being undermined. This is normal.

If you are comfortable with leading already, it is powerful to examine which kinds of leadership you use and when you use them. It is especially useful to notice when you switch styles. Do you use the control style of leadership when you are afraid or angry or with certain kinds of people? Where are you leading by demonstrating, and are there ways you can increase this style? Are there people you particularly want to empower? How do you want to empower them? Do you sell out on your leadership in certain situations? All these questions are useful for waking up out of the automatic nature of the models we live in.

If you are a novice at leading, it is powerful to make an assessment of where you are already leading by pioneering something new or demonstrating your integrity by speaking and acting in harmony with your results. The areas where you are leading do not have to be publicly acknowledged. For example, you might be leading in kindness in your church by demonstrating it to other congregants who are particularly difficult, or you might be leading by being someone who is masterful using a computer or by being someone who is great at connecting people. You can lead in hundreds of ways by pioneering and/or demonstrating even the smallest things that set you apart from the people around you. What I have found over nearly twenty-five years of working with people is that *every person is leading in some way in her or his life.* To wake up to the power of your own leadership is the thrill of a lifetime because it puts you in the driver's seat for the world you want and gives you the opportunity to take others with you.

New Realities

At the heart of this chapter is an idea that has the power to alter the way you live, even the course of your life. That idea is that what we call reality is a series of models or belief systems that shape the way we think, perceive, and experience ourselves and the world around us. Though most people are unconsciously competent with the systems of belief to which they adhere, very few have the conscious competence to change models or create new ones. People who do have this competence are called original thinkers, geniuses, or even dangerous radicals, depending on who is talking about them. It is sad to realize, but most people go through their lives never having an original thought. How they think, what they do and say, and the results they get in life are largely programmed by the models in which they live. Though we use the popular slogan "Think outside the box" to solve problems, few people have the power to think outside the box when it comes to changing models that threaten their preconceived view of themselves.

To begin to recognize that who you see yourself to be and what is available to you are simply products of models you hold can be joyous and exciting. It can also be challenging and scary. The actual process of seeing the model you live in and learning to alter it or invent a new one may take the kind of courage and persistence you think only other people have. One woman I know described this process as a "psychedelic experience." As I mentioned earlier, real leadership may lie in the willingness to question the realities in which you live.

In Chapter 3, the model called The Feminine Principle is examined in depth. Before going on, it might be worthwhile to re-read this chapter or sections of it and let yourself absorb the impact of this information at the emotional and physical level, as well as the intellectual level. As most people know, real learning takes intelligence that goes well beyond what is intellectual.

When the information in Chapter 2 takes root, it has the power to ground you in your ability to use the information from the rest of this book. The result can have you leading in every area of your life.

Chapter 3

Foundation of Genius: The Feminine Principle

The Feminine Principle model has the spirit of our humanity at its most generous and humane built right into it. It starts from the very point of view that humanity is trying so desperately to achieve. Its core reality is that human beings are essentially social, interdependent, and more alike than not. Practically speaking, The Feminine Principle model is stable enough to hold the aspirations of all human beings because it acknowledges relationship with every human being. It is also flexible enough to expand, change, and grow in ways that are essential if we are to create a world in which everyone would be happy to live. Women have a genius for expanding "family" to include in-laws, children, neighbors, and friends, regardless of their foibles and shortcomings.

Did you know that *genius* comes from an Arabic word that means "spirit"? Probably not; our educational model teaches us to think of genius as *intellectual brilliance* alone. However, you can think of a model as having a particular genius, meaning a spirit that permeates the point of view of the model. The spirit of The Masculine Principle is rugged individualism. The spirit of The Feminine Principle is relatedness and cooperation.

Across all cultures, women can be said to hold the spiritual values and behaviors that separate human beings from the animals around them. In fact, in most cultures, women are the primary transmitters of the values of the culture. They hold what might be called the heart and soul of the culture. Ironically, even in cultures where women are most devalued, it is usually the women who transmit the superior value of males and the inferior value of females to their children. For example, in cultures that practice female genital mutilation, the ritual is often performed by an older woman in the girl's family.

In Chapter 2, we explored what a model is and discovered its power to shape reality. In this chapter, we turn our attention to a specific model, The Feminine Principle, and examine its basic assumptions and core values, as well as its strengths and weaknesses. If we are to create a New Feminine Principle, it is vital to know and understand The Feminine Principle that we have inherited. As with any journey, you have to know where you are starting from if you want to get where you are going.

The Four Basic Assumptions

Discovering the assumptions of a model is like doing detective work. By examining how people who use the model operate and what they expect, you find clues to the basic construction of the model itself. The four basic assumptions of The Feminine Principle are what I see as its underlying structure. I identified them by listening to what women say about life and how they say it, and by observing what they do and how they do it. For example, when I was a boy, my mother, my brothers, and I would often take the subway downtown to go shopping. In the twenty minutes it took to get downtown, my mother would have struck up a conversation with another woman sitting near us, and they exchanged intimate information about their families, swapped stories about their church or their childhood, even consoled or advised each other about problems they were facing. By the time we got off the subway, my mother and the woman would have the feel of intimate friends, though they would probably never see each other again. This genius for instant relationship amazed me.

As I look back now, it is clear to me that my mother assumed that she had a relationship with everyone and everything around her. She also assumed that anyone with whom she spoke had things in common with her. She would never have said that everyone and everything is connected or that life is holographic at every level. That is my way of saying the first two basic assumptions of this model. My mother would have said, "You know, Bill, people are all just people."

The third basic assumption of The Feminine Principle, that the best strategy is one of wholeness, comes directly from the assumption that all life is connected. When things are connected they make a pattern, and viewed with enough scope, that pattern forms a unique design. As in the story of the blind men feeling an elephant, each man's report of the part he was feeling may have been accurate, but their overall conception of what an elephant really looked like was way off the mark. I have often heard women refer to the "web of Life," and have come to realize that in assuming that everyone and everything is connected, women also assume that those connections make a coherent picture. In the masculine style of thinking, things tend to be broken down into their smallest distinguishable parts. In the feminine style, there is more importance on building the big picture. Neither style is "wrong" and both styles have their place; however, the feminine style is what strategists call a global style because it paints a picture from many diverse pieces simultaneously. It is therefore more useful for a world that is getting smaller and more connected every minute.

The fourth basic assumption, which comes directly from the assumption that all life is connected and more alike than not, is that the world we want opens from The Feminine Principle. To be more accurate, you could even say that the world itself opens from The Feminine Principle, because it is in assuming connection that the world around you—and your place in it—comes into perceptual focus. People with severe autism lack this perceptual focus and live trapped in their individual worlds. You could call the fourth basic assumption the assumption of sociability and shared concerns, the starting point for living and working together to achieve what we want. In this last assumption, opportunities for group, unity, inclusion, co-creation, partnership, and celebration occur. Here the world that would be a pleasure for all humans finds life.

Finally, it is important to remember that the way this model
and its assumptions were created had nothing to do with the way I
am systematically ordering them. These assumptions more probably came out of the chaos of everyday life for millions of people,
women in particular, who passed down their experiences to their
daughters over hundreds of generations. I do not hold these assumptions as "true" in absolute terms. I do know that when I have
stated these assumptions to thousands of women over many years,
there has been instant recognition. In fact, my ability to present
them as four distinct assumptions is the result of the generosity of
scores of women who have been willing to educate me about the
place from which women think, not just what they think.

To create an innovation in any model, you have to understand
the structure of the model and use that as a reference point. The
Feminine Principle is the basic recipe for a great life. When you
add four key ingredients—capacity, truth, voice, and stance—to
the mix, you get a New Feminine Principle, a model that creates
the opportunity for wholeness in every human being.

One: Everyone and Everything Is Connected

You are standing at the kitchen sink one morning, finishing a glass
of juice. You are thinking about your best friend who lives in another state. You haven't heard from her this month and you decide
you will call her this evening when you have time to talk. You
smile at the thought of a leisurely chat, wash out your glass, and
head out the door. Ten minutes later, your cell phone rings. It is
your best friend. She says she has been thinking about you since
she awoke this morning. She apologizes for not being in touch
and invites you to have a long chat to catch up—maybe tonight, if
you're not busy. You laugh.

People have hundreds, even thousands of experiences like this
in the course of a lifetime. Normally, we call those experiences
"coincidences" because we cannot quite imagine that our "little"
thought standing at the kitchen sink could be received hundreds

or thousands of miles away. It might help to know that the Nobel Prize has been shared several times by laureates who were thinking the same thoughts and making the same discovery simultaneously in different parts of the world.

As the vice president in his team meeting discovered (in Chapter 2), you are as "in relationship" as it gets. The clothes you wear, the newspaper you read, the electricity that lights up your home, your home itself, the fillings in your teeth, all are a collective effort. Not only that. We are so in relationship to one another that you wouldn't even have survived the first few months of your life unless people acknowledged and acted on their connection with you.

The famous hundredth monkey studies of a few decades ago suggest that there is a species consciousness or connection that transcends location. When enough monkeys on one island learned to wash the potatoes that they had dug up in ocean water, monkeys on other islands suddenly started to do the same thing, apparently without firsthand knowledge of what the other monkeys had learned to do.

In 1983, before the public advent of the World Wide Web and widespread cellular technology, Peter Russell theorized the emergence of a "global brain." He predicted that when human population reached a critical mass, somewhere between six and twelve billion, there would be a global awakening in favor of unified human consciousness. His predictions are coming true even as we watch the developments that link us through live satellite TV broadcasts, high-speed transmission of information to millions of people on the web, and cellular networks that have the capability of reaching anyone anywhere in the world. The Live-Aid Concert twenty years ago, the first global TV event, launched an era in which the whole world is literally watching. If you watched the ringing in of the year 2000, you know that time zone by time zone for twenty-four hours, we were able to watch and be part of our fellow human beings celebrating the beginning of a new millennium.

   With the advent of these amazing events and with the continued development of unified field theory in physics, science has finally begun to acknowledge what women and mystics have asserted for thousands of years: life everywhere is connected. Everything you are and everything you do impacts life around you. It takes an immense leap of faith to imagine that your own life impacts life everywhere, though that is what scientists are finally acknowledging. Certainly, if you look at your own body, it is obvious that what you eat affects every part of you and an injury to any part of you affects your overall vitality. If you think of life at large as one "body," you can see how everything that goes on in that body affects it in some manner or other.

   When you compare the spirits of The Masculine and Feminine Principles, you discover a potential for more aliveness, vibrancy, and turn-on in The Feminine Principle. Living with the spirit of rugged individualism, many men have a tendency to hold themselves apart from life around them, all the while observing and analyzing it without a powerful experiential access to it. Certainly, The Loner, The Outlaw, The Rebel, and The Maverick—people who do not fit into society—are all central icons of masculine culture. On the other hand, living with the spirit of relatedness and cooperation, most women feel connected to the network of life around them because they experience it directly, through a model that gives them deep experiential access to it. What women and mystics may have in common is this direct experience of the connection of life. This is entirely different from the intellectual understanding of life often associated with male-dominated science models. In mysticism the experience of full connection is so all-encompassing that it is experienced as profound bliss and is said to activate the consciousness in ways that can never be reversed. To gain mastery of and lead in a model that produces the experience of bliss and vibrancy is a major access to power and personal fulfillment.

Two: Life Is Holographic at Every Level

When you adopt the first assumption of this model, you "know" that you are connected to everyone and everything. This is the first half of the core of The Feminine Principle—that we are all in it together and have a vested interest in having everyone win. What you might not know is that you are connected to billions of human beings who are nearly identical to you in every way (the second half of that core). Human DNA is more than 99 percent identical for all human beings. While men and women have different bodies, their basic human structure is more than 99 percent alike. Another way of saying this is that life is *holographic*.

Holograms were a breakthrough in visual technology. A hologram is made from more than a hundred photos of an object taken from every angle and then integrated by computer and printed on special materials. When you slice any part of the hologram and extract a piece, the entire picture is in the piece you took. Technical magic and a lot of fun!

This same principle applies to the little sugar cubes you put in your tea. Each and every cube of sugar contains the full essence or "picture" of sugar. In a large, five-pound block of sugar, the quantity would be more; however, the essence of sugar—what makes sugar, sugar—would be the same.

Although human beings come in all sizes, shapes, and colors, with myriad different cultural beliefs and practices, the essence of full humanity lives in each human being. This principle could also be called wholeness, meaning that what makes human beings human is intrinsically found in every human being, though it can be amplified, suppressed, or expressed in a staggering variety of beliefs, traditions, and behaviors.

In the 1950s, the U.S. government and press told Americans that the Russians were evil monsters who were only out to kill them. Russians were portrayed as being one step short of werewolves with blood dripping from their fangs. Only the U.S. government was fending off the onslaught of these dangerous, beast-like people. Ironically, the Russian people were also being told many of the same things about Americans by their government and press.

Then the Cold War thawed and Americans began to travel to Russia. Though the circumstances of life for Russian people were very different and often more difficult than our own, Americans were pleasantly shocked to realize that Russians were a lot like Americans in the most basic ways. They love their children, are afraid of nuclear war, and want a better quality of life for the next generation. They work, they socialize, and they laugh and cry. Their customs might be different, but their humanity is essentially the same. The lie of both governments was exposed.

What this means is that if you are human, you have the same basic equipment and concerns that *all* human beings have. When you want to know how another person feels or what she is experiencing, you can just put yourself in her place and imagine what you would feel. That's the right answer nearly all the time, because the other person's humanity is just like yours. Humanity is holographic in every human being. "Do unto others as you would have them do unto you"—a principle with which nearly every religion is imbued—is a straightforward piece of advice that is based on the principle that life is holographic. If it matters to you, you can bet it matters to other human beings, too.

Three: The Best Strategy Is One of Wholeness

It is fascinating to watch an infant. Her body may move in different directions simultaneously, the individual parts having no relation to one another. She has not yet learned to use her body in a coordinated manner. It's as if each arm and leg has a life of its own. After several months, a dramatic change occurs. Now the baby moves her arms and legs in harmony and all the parts of her body operate in a coordination that continues to develop and deepen through her childhood and adolescence. As an adult, she displays integration or *wholeness* in her physical expression.

If the first assumption of The Feminine Principle is connection, the assumption that the best strategy is one of wholeness is an acknowledgment that parts of the body not only connect, they unite to form something bigger than the sum of the parts. I have heard it said of a famous and beautiful actress that, taken individually, her facial features are not extraordinary, but viewed as a whole, her face is superb.

Using a different metaphor, if you could view your life as a company, you would see that you have many holdings, ventures, and departments that all work together and must be in harmony for your life to be "profitable." Your body is that way. There are myriad parts that must operate together for you to stay alive and go about the business of your life. Any simple action requires the simultaneous coordination of brain, nerves, organs, and muscles, not to mention the underlying processes of the body that you take for granted, such as breathing, blood flow, and digestion.

Because of the dominant (masculine) model's belief that nothing is essentially connected and holographic, many people live as if the various aspects of their lives are separate as well. Spirituality has nothing to do with sexuality. Business has nothing to do with personal life. Health has nothing to do with emotion.

Consider the performers in the circus who line up many sticks on a stand and spin plates on them. They put three or four plates up and get them going. Then they put four more plates up and spin them, while needing to go back to plates one through four, which by this time have begun to wobble. By plate number twelve, the ante is raised dramatically and this is where the fun for the audience really starts. These performers run back and forth along the line of plates, trying to keep them all spinning, while smiling at the audience as if nothing in particular were out of the ordinary.

Sound familiar? This is the way most human beings conduct "the business" of their lives because they live in a model that does not acknowledge that nourishing any aspect of life nourishes every aspect of life. Whichever plate has the biggest wobble gets the most attention. The strategy is to run back and forth spinning the plates as if they are all unrelated. It's an exhausting way to live, as anyone who has done it knows from personal experience. Things begin to wobble and crash. Maddening, and yet, like the performer spinning plates, you feel obligated to smile all the while and make it look easy.

In the face of a belief system that claims that life is not connected and holographic, there is an enormous pretense that the people who are juggling many different balls at the same time are better, more fulfilled, or even more talented than the rest of us. Their exhaustion is overlooked until something breaks down. Having had many intimate conversations with successful people, it is clear to me that the people who have real success are those who see the connection between all areas of their lives. They create strategies that are the equivalent of drilling a hole through all the plates and balancing them all on one stick.

In thousands of conversations with people from all walks of life, I have discovered that most people have areas of their life's "business" that are thriving. They also have areas that are just breaking even and areas that are so marginal that they really don't know what to do with them and often just try to ignore them.

To have a personal strategy that allows all the parts of your life to be nourished simultaneously would be a pioneering effort of major proportions … unless you live in a world (model) where life is connected and holographic.

Imagine a life where your spirit, intelligence, body, sexuality, emotion, and energy were engaged and operating harmoniously and with full capacity. Imagine a life where, as you nourished one aspect of your life, all the aspects were nourished. You would be a leading human, in the same way that any corporation that is functioning smoothly and making a handsome profit is a leading corporation. The Feminine Principle sets the stage for this. The New Feminine Principle makes it possible.

Four: The World We Want Opens from The Feminine Principle

When you consider what you get from a model of reality that is generated from the idea that life is connected and holographic, here is what you find:

1. Emphasis on what unites rather than what divides
2. Inclusion rather than exclusion
3. A sense of being in groups, in expanding circles of relatedness, from two or more to billions and billions
4. A preference for co-creation—the desire to cooperate with others to achieve commonly valued goals
5. A "one goes, all go" mentality
6. Maybe the most important—the possibility of the celebration of life, rather than the battle of it

All six results form the very basis for a viable, sustainable, and happy life for all human beings.

These are my basic findings when I examine The Feminine Principle as a starting point for a Principle of Wholeness. I invite you to find many more things that are useful and to express them in as many ways as possible. It is crucial to see the real, practical importance of this way of thinking, which has for the most part been relegated to family life with no connection to the world at large. It is also crucial to make the conscious connections that enable you to use this model everywhere. You can start from this model in your family and be a leading parent. You can start from it in your business and be a leading salesperson or a leading executive. You can start from The Feminine Principle in the political process and become a leading advocate for change.

You can start from the idea that life is connected and holographic in *any* role you play. In the same way that a method actor uses "The Method" to develop her roles, you can use The Feminine Principle to develop roles for every area of your life. When you develop roles that are free from the taint of the dominator model, you create a version of that role that is new, unique—one of a kind. Every time you do that, you are a pioneer, a leader. Every time you get results in that role in your own life, you lead by demonstration and open a possibility for other people in the same role to have their own unique version, making them pioneers. Every time you encourage others to make that same kind of leap, you are a leader of empowerment.

When you think like women in business who describe their businesses in family terms and when you apply that thinking globally, you see that the world's business is really a family business—the entrepreneurial endeavor of the family of humanity. Leadership that starts with The Feminine Principle and transcends home and family to make its power felt in the world at large may be the beginning of the answer to the problems we face on a global scale. When you add capacity, truth, voice, and stance to create a New Feminine Principle with wholeness built in, you also create a wave of original leadership that has the power to go beyond solving problems and start designing the world we want. The secret is to start by designing the world you want inside yourself and testing that design in your own life.

It is important to remember that the principles of "connected and holographic" have power by virtue of being beliefs with which millions and millions of people—especially women—agree. As with any belief system, when you take the stand that life is connected and holographic, you begin to gather evidence that it is true. So it is equally important to remind yourself that models are developed to explain, predict, and control phenomena. The real power of a model is not whether it is "true," but whether it is effective in getting results that are valuable to human beings.

If you stop now and look into your personal desires and concerns (what is valuable to you), you will discover that what you want for children—yours, mine, theirs, girls, boys, black, white, Muslim, Jewish—is a world in which there is a real chance for a viable, sustainable, and happy life. You also want that for yourself, though you may despair of ever having it, based on the way the world is now. That desire is undeniable because it is imbedded in the hologram of our humanity. Imagine if you can that you would hesitate even for a moment to help any child in danger. Impossible. The common humanity you share overrules any other differences. In fact, at that moment those differences are trivialized to nearly nothing. Like electricity, the power of human relatedness has gigantic "voltage" and can be harnessed to light up humanity in ways that we have barely begun to explore.

The Four Core Values of The Feminine Principle

The French people refer to *la vrai France*, "the true France," as the areas of France and the way people live in those areas that are the real expression of what is at the heart of being French. In the United States, we say a person, a thing, or an experience is "the real deal" or "the gold standard" to indicate that it is worthwhile and has intrinsic value at the highest level. The shared experiences of women throughout the ages create a background against which women from all cultures and classes have found intrinsic value and pleasure in living their lives. These experiences have become the recognized gold standard for the vast majority of women.

If the four basic assumptions of The Feminine Principle create the model itself, the four core values can be seen as the source of the experiences that created the assumptions in the first place. While The Feminine Principle is a system of belief, not a fixed gender trait, it is obvious that women have similar experiences on which they place enormous value, such as the miraculous experience of giving birth or the power of cooperating with the birthing process. The biological imperative to nourish children and create a sustaining environment for them is nearly universal among women. These and other powerful experiences have helped to shape the assumptions that The Feminine Principle holds to be true.

The core values of The Feminine Principle are the real deal for people who "think" in this model—whether they are women or men—and they are readily recognizable to anyone who lives in this model. These core values not only orient you to The Feminine Principle model; they also point to the landmark experiences that make the model truly valuable. Moreover, if you interviewed hundreds of women (as I have), you would find that most women could identify these values without knowing the assumptions of the model. In a figure/ground relationship, the four core values are the figure and the assumptions the background against which you see them.

Cooperation Creates and Sustains Life

Cooperation is the principle on which all life hinges. Human beings cannot survive unless they are cared for around the clock for their first several years. Nobody gets through life on their own.

Until the 1960s, the word *ecology* was virtually unknown by all but the most educated or dedicated people. As a world, we had no working relationship with the idea that what we dumped into the ocean in one part of the world poisoned millions of people, animals, or plants in other parts of the world. In fact, the popular myth was that the oceans were inexhaustible and could handle anything we put into them. That might have been true in the agricultural age, but not the industrial age.

As individuals, we also had no relationship with our bodies as a unified environment, with an ecosystem all its own. Until recently the term *holistic medicine* was not in the popular culture, and practitioners of healing arts outside of the Western medical model were considered quacks. The medical model was famous for reporting patients as "the gallbladder in Room 2-A," with no relationship to the person who owned that particular organ.

For all mammals, including human beings, the most fundamental act of creation is an act of cooperation between two. Though breakthroughs in the science of cloning may change that in the near future, for the moment and for all of our history, it is this cooperation between a man and a woman and between two sets of chromosomes that has allowed us to survive and flourish. Cooperation is what creates.

At the macro level of life, it is the "cooperation" between the sun and the earth that creates an environment for organic life. The cooperation between plants and humans provides oxygen that sustains humans and carbon dioxide that sustains plants. Cooperation between countries with raw materials and manufacturing countries enables the manufacture of countless products that enrich our lives. Cooperation not only creates; it creates more.

At the micro level, cooperation between the organ systems of our bodies keeps us alive and healthy. The microscopic plant and animal life in our intestines help digest the food that we supply, enabling all of us to live and grow. Cooperation is what creates more and sustains life at every level.

If you have ever worked on a team—and we all have at one time or another—you know that it is the willingness of team members to cooperate that makes all the difference in getting the quality of results you want and in the quality of your experience working on a team. Ever been on a team where someone is trying to be the star player? That's one experience. Ever been on a team that operates as a single organism? That's quite another experience.

Because of our belief in Rugged Individualism, we live in a cultural model where there is an enormous pretense of going it alone. Like the corporate vice president mentioned in Chapter 2, people who live with this belief have the experience of not being essentially related to anyone or anything around them. In psychiatry, people who lose this fundamental ability to experience connection are called psychopathic, autistic, or schizophrenic, depending on the behaviors they display.

Take a moment and do this simple visualization to feel the power of cooperation. Imagine yourself standing under a nice hot shower with plenty of water. As you are enjoying the hot water, you think of the people who made the hot water heater and all the people who supplied parts and technology to build it and you thank them. You also think about the people who ran the tubing through your house that carries the water, and the people who made the tubing, and the people who mined the copper for the tubing, and the people who transported the copper and the finished tubing, and you thank them. Then you think about the people at the utility companies who supply the water for your shower and the gas to heat it. You also think about the people who manage the water supply in your area and the people who are responsible for the water quality. To your delight you realize that there are thousands and thousands, if not millions and millions, of people who cooperated so you could take your shower. Cooperation is what creates more and sustains life—yours, mine, everyone's.

Of course you could find your own water and find a way to heat it and rig up a way to wash. Millions of people have to do that every single day. The question is not of ability, but quality. When people cooperate, the "more" that is created is increased quality of life and convenience. Your safety net broadens and gets stronger. Things are easier. They are also a lot more fun.

At the spiritual level, co-creation has come to mean cooperating with a larger "spirit of life" to create and manifest your desires. You certainly experience that when you procreate children. You and your mate may engage sexually, but the actual process of fertilization is a mysterious process that is describable but not explainable. Though we certainly know the stages that a fetus goes through, we have no real idea what actually makes a tiny cell become a human being in the exact order of development that every other human being goes through. One thing is abundantly clear. Something is creating within you that knows exactly how to do it. To tap into that creative source within you may be the most powerful form of cooperation available.

Birth, Nourishment, and Growth Are Life's Basic Pleasures

Riane Eisler's research indicates that in the earliest cultures, where people worshipped the Goddess, giving birth was the chief godly power because it was an expression of pure creation. In agrarian cultures, the feminine aspect of God was also seen to give birth to the crops and animals that were the very life of the people. These cultures enjoyed a gentle and more equitable way of life.

All that changed with the coming of the hordes that swept across Europe from the East, bringing with them the worship of the god of war, a stern, masculine deity who demanded living sacrifices. The power that women have to give birth was eclipsed by the power that men have to bring death. This worship of death continues today in the glorification of martyrs, in the graphic accounts of death by our news media, and by our morbid fascination with serial killers and other agents of death and destruction.

Be that as it may, the most glorious event in any family is the birth of a child. Well over 90 percent of the women and men I have interviewed report the birth of their children as the first or second most significant event in their lives.

At the moment you see your child, you make a promise, whether spoken or not, that you will do everything in your power to sustain her. Food, clothing, shelter, love, and education—whatever she needs, you promise to provide. This drive is so strong that when a woman who is breastfeeding hears her baby cry—or any baby for that matter—her breasts begin to leak milk. Even when parents do not live up to the promise of sustenance for their children, they feel that drive. It is part of being human.

You also discover another promise that is equally true. As you hold your child, you promise to do everything in your power to have your child go beyond you and have a better life than you had. This promise can readily be seen in immigrants who have gone without things for themselves so their children could have a chance to do better than they did.

Though we are taught to honor people who nourish their children at their own expense, there is a strong element of sacrifice that is not consistent with the true feminine spirit of nourishment. It clearly violates the "one goes, all go" rule of The Feminine Principle. In terms of leadership, children are much better served if their parents demonstrate their own nourishment and growth and use that as a model to teach their own children to nourish themselves and grow. Otherwise, the cycle of sacrifice—so identified with the worship of death—continues and is passed down from generation to generation.

Whether you do it with a child, a garden, a personal vision, an invention, or a project, birth, nourishment, and growth are holographic to every aspect of life. Taken together, they are life's greatest pleasures because they are what move life forward and expand it. When you give birth to leadership in yourself and nourish it, you grow and mature and give birth to others' leadership, who in turn grow and mature and give birth to others'. Of such, new worlds are made.

The process of taking nourishment is so imbedded in the human psyche that almost every important human event and ritual is accompanied by food—often by feasting. Nutritionists say that strong cravings for a particular kind of food often signify the body's need for the nutrients found in that food. It is a wonderful fact of our biology that when you give yourself what really nourishes you, your enjoyment is dramatically enhanced.

The process of digesting a good meal is one of life's most intrinsic pleasures. You feel a pleasant glow after you have eaten well. The feeling of being full and well nourished enables you to savor what you have without regard to what comes next. The future and the past fade, and the enjoyment of present time expands. This is similar to the glow people feel after great sex.

This savoring of any aspect of your life can be a high-level spiritual practice of being grateful in the moment. In the world of consciousness, nothing facilitates savoring more than gratitude.

Gratitude comes from the Latin word *gratia*, mean
"thanks." To be grateful is literally to be full of grac
nourished with grace. It is the mental equivalent of now ,
physically after a great meal. Gratitude is the digestive juice of
consciousness and enables you to have more by acknowledging
and enjoying—digesting—what you have.

In the world of public honors, honoree acceptance speeches are
almost entirely expressions of gratitude to the people who made
the honor possible. It is the only way to digest the large "meal"
that they have been given. As you digest anything, physically or
mentally, you nourish yourself. The natural expression of nourishment is growth.

One way to continue to grow all your life is to give birth to
new ways to think, new ways to live, new projects, new friendships, new levels of responsibility, or new expressions of yourself
and to continue to nourish what you have given birth to. To be
grateful in the form of acknowledging what you have accom-
plished, who you have become, or how you have empowered others is to learn the art of sustainable growth.

Some people say that life is a circle; however, when you give
birth to, nourish, grow, and enjoy your creations, you discover
that life is not a circle but a spiral. Each turn of the spiral takes
you to a new level from which you can more expansively give birth
to your creations.

The fountain of youth resides in your ability to give birth not
just to your children and your ideas, but to yourself over and over,
to discover who you are and nourish it in each new chapter. Nothing could be more pleasurable. Nothing could be more feminine.

To Open and Include More Is the Essence of What Is Feminine

Everyone knows women who are "gatherers." They include more
and more people simply because they have a vast ability to expand
their capacity for relationship. In fact, they take pleasure in it.

These women create groups of affinity as they go. They make you feel that there is always room for one more person to pull up a chair and join in. As leaders of home and family, they make neighborhoods that are a pleasure to live in. In business, they create powerful teams that have a high degree of loyalty and cohesion. They may or may not have a coherent vision and a use for the team around them. What they do have is the instinct for relatedness and inclusion.

Mary Elizabeth lives in a small town in Northern California. When I first met her, she hired me to coach her in her expression of leadership in her community and in the larger community of women working on global issues. Mary Elizabeth invited me to visit her and her husband and daughters in their beautiful home in the Sierra foothills. There we talked about what it would be like for a community of 2,500 people—the size of her town—to be completely related and working together to have the quality of life they wanted. The townspeople had already worked on issues that threatened the whole community, like the damming of their local river.

Mary Elizabeth got excited about the idea of a town where The Feminine Principle was the model of choice and invited me to teach an intensive, six-month course about it in her town. She and her husband invited people to meet me, and we quickly had a full course. In the next six months, there were five more. At the end of four years, more than 200 people from her community had taken this intensive course and were a solid community of people who could think The Feminine Principle. They raised money for causes they believed in. They backed and worked to elect candidates who would protect their environment. Some of them went into business together; others did spiritual practices together, worked on improvement projects in one another's homes, or created celebrations and parties that seem to go on and on. They became in microcosm a brilliant example of what humanity could be in macrocosm. Everyone who came in contact with them wanted what they had. Mary Elizabeth's husband had been married twice before, and his relationship with his ex-wives was distant. When he was diagnosed with terminal cancer, she decided that he deserved to leave this world with his family relationships intact. She opened herself and reached out to his ex-wives and their children and galvanized this fractured family into a seamless unit. When her husband died, I experienced a moment of real jealousy. "This is the way I want to go," I thought, "surrounded by people who love me and who love one another, everything from the past healed and complete, and every family member a part of something bigger and stronger that can hold them and nurture them." The family that Mary Elizabeth opened herself to and gathered continues today.

The ability to open to the world around you is clearly a reflection of the ability to open to the internal process of life. There are situations that require us to open as the one and only solution. Whether it is opening to a new chapter of life or a new idea, or opening your heart to forgive someone, opening is the one and only effective solution.

Though it sometimes works for lids on cans, forcing or prying is a bad idea for people. As with flowers, opening comes from within and expresses itself by expanding into the world as blooming. When you open to a new idea, a new solution, or a new perspective, you get an epiphany, a "eureka!" moment, where suddenly the world makes sense in ways that it did not before. Things that were previously murky or obscure come into focus.

If I look for logical reasons why women are so good at opening, I can't help but notice it is the way they are built to operate. Women open their bodies to their partners to express sexuality. They open again to give birth. When more children come along, they open to give them the love they need to develop and grow. I don't really know if these reasons are "true." They are just things I have made up to explain this amazing quality of opening that lives for the most part in women and is clearly an integral part of the model they use. Maybe the reason is as simple as women's holding relatedness to be the central fact of life, and maintaining the view that they can increase their personal power by having more relatedness.

Opening and letting more in is a form of nourishment, a feminine quality that can empower leadership everywhere. It may be the single most creative power that women possess, in that it makes available new avenues, pathways, and possibilities where none existed before. Inventions and leaps forward live in the province of the open mind.

One beautiful metaphor for the feminine way of opening is the image of a pebble dropped into a pond. The pebble sinks to the bottom and remains there, but waves of energy open out from the point of contact, making bigger and bigger circles that include more and more of the pond. Maybe you don't have to go charging around to get things done. Maybe all you need to do is stay where you are and open to more. Consider never having to muscle your way through to a result ever again. Imagine that everything you've ever wanted could be made available simply by opening yourself to new views of yourself, new information, new relationships, new experiences, and new ways to express yourself. That would be a form of powerful magic.

Now, imagine for a moment a world where the women and men who have the ability to keep opening themselves and gathering others for the pleasure of relationship were allowed to operate at a global level with a common vision of discovering how to have the world we all desire. That would be co-creation at the highest level. Things would change in a hurry.

Style Is Just as Important as Result

Joan Holmes is an amazing woman. The president of The Hunger Project, a global organization whose mission is to alter the model in which we view hunger so that we can finally end it, she embodies the importance of style. In 1977, when The Hunger Project was inaugurated, the world lived in a model where hunger was inevitable, where there would never be enough, and where there were no solutions to the problem.

When I became a volunteer at The Hunger Project headquarters in San Francisco in 1979, I was stunned to see how beautiful everything was. Not only was the project housed in a donated Victorian mansion, but also there were wonderful arrangements of fresh flowers. The people who worked there dressed beautifully. They had the latest technology of every sort at their disposal. I immediately saw all of this as a waste of money that could better have been spent feeding the poor, even though Joan kept telling us that our job was to create the global will (or consciousness) to end hunger, not to do relief work.

One day in a meeting of staff and volunteers, I screwed up my courage and asked Joan about this shameful waste of money. I asked her how in good conscience she could spend resources to make the place look beautiful. Why did people have to look like movie stars? Was all this cutting-edge technology really necessary?

Joan is one of the most masterful and gracious women on earth. She thanked me for my question and then explained that if you are working on the issue of hunger and starvation day in and day out, the last thing in the world you should do is starve yourself. Then you are of no use to anyone.

She went on to say that everything in the environment of The Hunger Project was designed to reflect the style in which the world would conduct itself when hunger had ended, so that people could see now what that would look like. In other words, the style in which the result was being produced was just as important as the result itself. The envisioned result was the "what." The style was the "how." This was my first education in first-class style.

I have a friend who is a wedding planner. She told me that most couples are perfectly capable of planning their own wedding and doing a good job of it. "That's not what they hire me for. People hire me because they know I'll walk them through the planning and the wedding day itself in a style that leaves them able to enjoy what should be one of the most joyous days of their lives. In fact, some of my clients have told me they have used my style to handle big projects at work and have gotten them done elegantly, with a minimum of fuss. One of my brides," she said, "told me that she went from administrative assistant to office manager because her employer was so impressed with her work style." Style without results is empty and irrelevant. Results without style are a compromise. Results with style are the stuff of mastery.

A Closer Look at Style

Imagine you are invited to a State dinner at The White House. Heads of State, celebrities, and movers and shakers of all kinds will be in attendance. You start preparing from the moment you receive the invitation. You get advice on appropriate dress, allocate money for a new outfit, and enjoy every minute shopping for it. You get your hair, nails, and makeup done. You might even hire a limousine for the evening. Additionally, you might get instruction about protocol and etiquette, learn about the history of The White House, and get briefed on who will attend. No detail is too small. You know that this is a first-class event and you plan to arrive in style and enjoy it all the way through.

Most people could rise to the occasion of one night at this level. Now imagine living every single day of your life this way, taking the time and attention to make your life a first-class affair. After all, isn't your own life worth at least as much as a State dinner?

Most people think it takes a lot of money to live this way. Actually, it takes a lot of telling the truth about your own value as a human being and setting a standard for living that reflects that value. It also takes paying attention to the details of your life and how you operate in it. For most people, it is just too much trouble.

Let's face it—we are a "get it done" culture. We want results and we want them now, no matter what it costs or what gets left out. Congress spends enormous time and money fixing things that "got done," but were later found to be shoddy, incomplete, and poorly thought out. In the personal sphere, when "get it done" costs your sense of joy or your quality of life, you feel compromised.

Built into The Feminine Principle is a profoundly wise value, namely, that the style is just as important as the result. To imbue your life with a style that sustains you and gives you a full measure of happiness may be the most important personal investment you can make.

Sustained Results

As you know, many people can hit a target once. In the music industry, they are called "one-hit wonders." Hitting it over and over is another question. In the matter of The Hunger Project, the project goal is the sustainable end of hunger—i.e., not for one year, but year after year, forever. If you were trying to end hunger for one year only, you could use up all your resources to do it, but then you wouldn't be able to do it again next year. It is therefore important to develop a style that reflects the result you want *over time*. When the style in which you produce a result is consistent with the result itself, your ability to produce that result over and over is assured. If you want first-class results, it is good to develop a first-class style; if sustainable results, then a sustainable style; if beautiful results, then a style where beauty is built in. This takes the kind of intelligence that invents as it goes.

Are you one of those people who makes her house beautiful for guests, but not for herself? Do you take the time to put something you've picked up for dinner on a plate, or is it okay to eat it right out of the container? Have you bought flowers for yourself lately, or is that something you do for other people? Do you let your employer know how much you appreciate your job, or do you complain that your employer doesn't notice you enough? Have you ever argued with yourself over spending $1 more for better-quality tomatoes, when you have just spent $5 on an expensive coffee drink?

You are not right or wrong if you do the things I've mentioned. What is important to realize is that if you achieve your results in a graceful, feminine style, you will have that style imbedded in your results and increase your chances of getting those results more easily and more often. Feminine style is first-class style because it is cooperative, inclusive, nourishing, and acknowledging—even beautifying. It leaves its recipients open and receptive to more.

Many years ago when I had just arrived in San Francisco, I shared a flat with a striking woman who loved fashion and dressed accordingly. One day Rachel came home from an outlet store with a beautiful sweater. It came from a fine, high-end store and had been marked down nearly 90 percent. She was quite excited. As she showed me the sweater, she said, "This is a $400 sweater from I. Magnin. I got it for $49."

Being a man who was completely naïve and obviously liked to live dangerously, I casually mentioned that what she had bought was a $49 sweater. Rachel became upset and showed me the price tag to prove I was wrong. "There is no intrinsic value to anything," I replied smugly. "What makes an I. Magnin sweater worth $400 is not just the sweater itself, but dressing up and shopping at a beautiful store where you are treated like a queen, where your merchandise is carefully wrapped, and where you are given free samples of expensive perfumes. Instead, you went to a basement outlet, where you shopped for picked-over merchandise in an overcrowded store with harsh lighting and exposed plumbing." Needless to say, although I made my point, Rachel and I didn't last long as flat-mates. Heavy-handed and self-righteous style does not make for sustainable, enjoyable relationships.

Success at Any Price

Because no one sees the principle of style and results as being full partners, the way you produce results does not have to match in any way the results you want to produce. Have a sales target for your company this quarter? It's fine to work yourself into the ground to make it. Want to get your family fed in a hurry? It's fine to patronize fast-food chains whose food provides minimum nourishment. Want to make a lot of money? It's fine to spend less and less time with your kids. Want to excel in sports? It's okay to take steroids to increase performance and anesthetics to numb the pain so you can keep going. Long-term viability be damned!

Unless you recognize a relationship between the way you produce your result and the quality of the result, the probability of having full enjoyment of your result is reduced in direct proportion to the compromises you make along the way. Do the math. You have just made senior VP in your company. To do that, you have worked 70-hour weeks for the last ten years. You take a high blood pressure medication and a mild antidepressant, because the pressures at work are, to use appropriate jargon, killer. You have missed 63 soccer games with your kids, 1,523 evening meals with your family, 251 weekends at home, and 4,356 hours of sleep that have thrown your immune system off, causing you to have chronic low-grade infections. You have had just twelve weeks off in ten years and you took your business laptop with you on vacation. Welcome to the world where style has no essential relationship to the result. By the way, congratulations on your promotion!

Most of the models we live in now are the result of men thinking in models of winning wars. After all, this is how men have been trained for millennia. Because men have traditionally been the public presence of family groups, it stands to reason that business, politics, religion, sports, and other male-dominated activities would be imbued with the spirit of war. War, by definition, is a state of emergency. In a state of emergency, people are permitted to get things done in ways that would not be permitted in times of peace. Loss of life, crippling injuries, irreparable damage to human treasures, and destruction of the environment are all considered bearable costs in a state of war. The success of the military campaign reigns supreme. Unfortunately, this style of producing results has carried over into our culture at large. "Hostile take-overs" and "corporate raids" give you a good idea of the model being used.

This military style has far-reaching consequences for a culture that values success at any cost. This is winning with a discount. It may be successful, but it is hardly fulfilling. It is also a way of operating that burns out your adrenals and never gives you full enjoyment. It certainly is not a way to live everyday life. It kills off the vitality of the body and deadens the soul.

It is important to realize that success-based thinking is not essentially "male." It is a function of the "dominate or be dominated" version of The Masculine Principle. Unfortunately, winning any way you can lives in a model that presumes men are just that way. It is a model that traps and kills men by the millions. The power of models to create and reinforce reality is staggering even unto death.

When something is achieved at a ruinous cost, it is called a pyrrhic victory. Pyrrhus, the king of Epirus, was so intent on winning his wars with Rome that he used up and destroyed the wealth and resources of his own country. Success at any cost is a pyrrhic victory; it uses up resources at rates that are not tolerable, let alone sustainable.

For ten years I was a psychotherapist. I worked with people who were what psychotherapists at that time called "normal neurotic." Several years into my practice, I discovered something that changed everything. I discovered that the basic problem most people had was that they were living lives that were too small for them. Either their visions and desires were too small to have a really great life or they had compromised their visions and desires and were living at a discount. Sometimes they had the vision and desire but had developed a style of thinking that kept them at a level that was smaller than their aspirations.

I announced to my clients that I was unwilling to work on their problems anymore and that all I wanted was to speak with them about their aspirations and to coach them to live in a style that was consistent with realizing those aspirations. This was a radical departure from the style I had learned, which entailed focusing on my clients' problems. Surprisingly, they were relieved. Miraculously, many of the problems for which they had sought therapy disappeared when they realized that a new, expanded vision and a style to match it were all it took to get back on track. There wasn't anything to fix, just something to learn and get good at.

From Coach to First Class

About ten years ago I coached a woman, Roberta, whose style with her employees made them a first-class team. Roberta was a Human Resources executive for a major company. Her team was composed of people who were the backbone of her employee-benefits support team, but were not considered executive level and were overworked and overlooked. When a major change in employee benefits was put on the books, it was Roberta's team who would bear the brunt of the change and be deluged with calls from employees wanting to know what to do.

Roberta realized that her team was under enormous pressure that was not likely to let up anytime soon. She made a remarkable suggestion to her boss, the head of Human Resources. She suggested taking her employees for two days of meetings before the launch of the new benefits program. Her boss readily agreed and offered the company's conference room. Then Roberta told her boss that she was planning to take her employees to a beautiful resort hotel on the ocean, where they could have their meetings and have some fun. Her boss told Roberta that this was highly irregular, because the employees in question were not executive staff. Roberta did not budge.

She and I planned the meetings. Her people stayed in beautiful rooms that overlooked the ocean. We had lunch catered each day out on the patio. The meetings were scheduled for two hours in the morning and two in the afternoon. Evenings were free. We asked her team to work as a unit and produce a day's worth of work in a half-day. We told them that we wanted them to enjoy the resort and that we had big results we wanted to produce. We asked her team to invent new ways to work together that would make things go smoothly.

The meetings exceeded our expectations. The energy and cooperation of Roberta's team made them a pleasure. When we finished each day around 3:00 P.M., we invited her employees to meet at 8:00 P.M. for dinner. We encouraged them to do whatever they wanted to do between our meeting and dinner, including nothing at all if that's what they would like. We wanted them to discover a first-class style of working that was also a pleasure.

At the closing session of our meetings, one woman summed it up beautifully. "Roberta treated us like first-class employees," she said. "She taught us a style that we can pass on to the hundreds of employees who will be calling us about their new benefits. Also, when problems come up on our team—as they will—we have a powerful relationship with one another that will let us get things handled with a minimum of fuss."

When style and results go hand in hand, the quality of the result increases and the wear and tear on the people producing the result goes way down. That is first-class playing.

When you operate as if life is connected and holographic, in a style that values cooperation and inclusion, that follows the basic processes and pleasures of life—birth, nourishment, and growth—and that promotes greater opening and capacity, you are embodying and leading in The Feminine Principle.

Pluses and Minuses

It is important to keep reminding yourself that all models are simply inventions of human beings. Like any human invention,

The Feminine Principle has strengths and weaknesses. When you forget that a model is an invention and come to believe that whatever is represented in the model is "just the way it is," you lose your power over the model and give it power over you. What's left is submitting, rebelling, or walking away from the model, rather than changing it to reflect where you are now.

To create a New Feminine Principle, you need to have a clear view of the upside and downside of The Feminine Principle that we have inherited. Nothing is wrong and there is nothing to defend. It's more like going through Grandma's attic after she's gone and deciding what to keep and what to give away.

The Plus Side of The Feminine Principle

What makes The Feminine Principle valuable as a starting point is its focus on creating, nurturing, and sustaining relationship. Within the model, women network, partner, ask for help, and share the credit, making them outstanding team players. Women think together in dialogue. Women have the ability to focus on intangible as well as physical results, enabling them to make a more fully articulated plan and create a style of getting results that is graceful and sustainable and a lot more enjoyable. Living in relatedness, women also have the ability to see the other person's point of view, to create added value and to make agreements that are mutually satisfying, promoting loyalty and giving them a big advantage in long-term partnerships of every kind. All this comes from a single assertion that has been handed down from mother to daughter for thousands of years, namely that life is connected and holographic—though each woman would say it in her own unique way.

Women in general are more emotionally open and well nourished than men because they relate to all the aspects of their humanity. They provide the heart and soul and joy in most cultures. They have emotion as a value of relationship and they feel deeply. They are given this by The Feminine Principle in which they live.

You might ask how they escape the starvation that men live in. Women generally are not required to go into combat, a singular advantage over men. In war, men are forced to suppress their natural human emotional response in order to kill to win, a behavior that is so abhorrent that many men in war never get over it. In the culture at large, combat behavior translates into a fierce, "last man standing" competitiveness that values only winning without regard to the method or consequences of the win.

Women open their bodies for intercourse and birth, which enables them to experience the power and pleasure of being open and encourages them to stay that way. Also, because the job of women traditionally has been to raise children and create family, most cultures allow women a kind of emotional freedom, especially at home, that men do not experience. More than half a century ago, studies of institutionalized babies showed that without touching or some sense of emotional connection, many babies stopped growing. Some even died. A culture that required women to be as closed-hearted as men would disappear for lack of viable human beings to transmit it.

Because women carry a model of relatedness, they bring a host of valuable talents and skills to the table. Women think globally; that is, they possess an ability to include many, often contradictory, points of view, because they think in a model of relatedness. Women are famous for multitasking. Women display a heightened sense of intuition, a gift that seems particularly centered in emotion, something with which women have more freedom. Women are the carriers of spirituality. Though most religions suppress and discriminate against women to keep them out of power in the religious hierarchy, these same religions would go out of business without the support of women who form the bedrock of desire for spiritual expression. Spirituality, a sense of being connected to something bigger, is natural in a model of relatedness.

The Minus Side of The Feminine Principle

Though I have said it before, it bears repeating that the components of The Feminine Principle are not "true"; they are, however, real. What I mean is that any model, this one included, states its beliefs as if they are an absolute truth—just the way it is with no exception. This is the power and often the arrogance of holding a belief. On the other hand, when a belief is held and validated by millions of people over a long period of time, that belief gains the power of reality. People act as if the belief is true. When people act as if a belief is true and forget that it is simply a belief that can be changed at any time, their ability to evolve and grow as needed is limited. This single factor has caused more conflict, death, and destruction than any other cause in history. You can see this glaringly in religious cultures that barely tolerate people with other spiritual beliefs.

The Feminine Principle itself is a beautiful, powerful, and effective belief system. Sadly, it has been overlaid with dominator thinking. Although we might believe that this dominator mentality came from men, in truth we have no way of knowing how it actually started and who is responsible for it. Our best hypotheses are really only our best guesses.

When you look at Dr. Eisler's extensive research, what can be seen readily is that dominator thinking has torqued The Feminine Principle in particular ways that hobble it and rigidly control its power. This twisted version of The Feminine Principle has gained acceptance as The Feminine Principle itself, and has become the model for women through the power of tradition. There are three major ideas that overlay and distort The Feminine Principle and cause women to lose power:

1. Women's power is appropriate for and limited to household and family affairs.
2. Women's appetites and desires are appropriately voiced only for others, not for themselves.
3. Women are second-class human beings.

Women live in a world where the model they hold is not valued except in rigidly controlled circumstances, particularly home and family. In a world that has traditionally been dominated by the superior physical power of men, The Masculine Principle that "nothing is essentially connected and holographic" has become the standard. This creates the perception in men's minds that how and what women think is, by definition, not first class or up to standard.

The mindset of the "second class-ness" of women is one of the most pervasive mindsets throughout the world. In Africa, where women raise 80 percent of the food, they are given 10 percent of the subsidies. In the United States, women-owned businesses receive 5 percent of all the money invested each year, though women-owned businesses are the fastest-growing segment of American business.

Most women lack a feeling of freedom, power, safety, and control over their lives. Although women are often seen primarily as their bodies, often it is men who own those bodies. Historically, the value of women's virginity was its proof that "the goods" had not been damaged or "the breeding stock" had not been contaminated. Through the centuries women have been suppressed, owned, and killed with virtual impunity because they have been viewed as possessions of men. Five thousand bride burnings continue to occur in India each and every year. Most of the one billion people who go to bed hungry each night are children and women. Ironically, malnourished women give birth to malnourished children and the next generation is weakened in every way.

A woman leader I know spoke eloquently about her realization that, for the culture in which she lives, her own "personal pathology" was her gender. She said that when she realized she would never be able to "fix" this pathology, the feeling she had was one of despair, followed by a determination to have a world in which women are first class. Living in a model of relatedness as she does, she also went on to say that her vision is that both women and men are first-class human beings.

Women often find themselves easily desiring the best for others (relatedness), while lacking a clear voice for their own desires and best interests (individuality). Women clearly influence decisions, though they may not necessarily have practice wielding their own personal power in ways that would allow them to make command decisions. Women have traditionally been seen as the power behind the throne, not the one sitting on the throne itself. Women who lack the confidence and training to wield power at higher levels of risk and achievement limit their own effectiveness.

No less an organization than the United Nations has proclaimed that the *key* missing ingredient for the solution of the world's problems is to unleash the voice and the power of women. The only way to do that is one by one by one.

It is also no secret that women are without a full voice for the world they want, even their own safety and the ability to extend that safety to their daughters. Estimates are that one hundred million women have had their clitorises removed in the name of tradition. For the most part, these genital mutilations have been performed by other, older women who have gone through the same torture in the name of "that's just the way it is to be a woman" and who want their girl children to be seen as "real" women by the culture in which they live.

In order to make effective change, you first need to know what you are dealing with. By now you should have a good sense of the way models operate and the way The Feminine Principle model as we now know it operates. The rest of this book is devoted to giving you principles and tools that elevate The Feminine Principle to a new level of power and effectiveness, free from the domination of the past. These keys have the power to bring a New Feminine Principle into focus, seated in relationship, enriched by first-class style, and with the ability to create and sustain wholeness. Enjoy it. It is what you were born for.

Chapter 4

The Key of Full Capacity

Capacity, the first key to the New Feminine Principle, comes from a root word that means "able to hold much" or "spacious." It refers to an ability to contain large amounts with plenty of room to operate. We all know people like that. They operate in a style that enables people around them to relax, be themselves, and feel that everything is under control. Reverend Sofreeyah, a television personality in New York, is just like that. Everywhere she goes, she touches people in ways that give them more room to operate. At lunch one day our waiter was surly and abrupt. I wanted to ask for another waiter, but Reverend Sofreeyah put her hand on my arm and said, "Bill, give me a moment with him." The next time the waiter came to the table, she smiled at him and said, "Tough day, huh?" She was genuinely interested and her interest disarmed him. He took a few moments to say why he was having a bad day and even laughed. She thanked him for his service, which improved dramatically for the rest of our meal.

At the heart of the New Feminine Principle is the ability to expand your capacity to include more in your own life and the lives of people around you. For millennia, women have been forced into roles that are second class. They have also been coerced into silence or submission by the masculine dominator culture. Fortunately, the freedom to be great and to operate openly is growing rapidly. To have that freedom is one thing; to be able to use it fully is another. Most people know that a person who has been bedridden for many months has to rebuild the capacity to walk. People who have not exercised for a long time must build a capacity for exercise gradually. It is useful to consider that what is seen as a "normal" capacity for leadership may not have anything to do with what you are really capable of. Building a brand-new capacity for enjoyment, for saying what is on your mind, for ending compromises in which you live, for using power brilliantly, and for being a person who commands respect for who you really are is the key to living a first-class life.

Building a capacity to hold more and more of the "voltage" that comes with being a sovereign woman—that is, a woman at the center of her own life, in full power—makes all the difference between being electrified or electrocuted. In the 1950s when I was growing up, most houses had wiring that held 60 amps of electrical capacity. As people bought more electrical devices, they soon discovered that using the hair dryer and toaster at the same time often blew a fuse. Within a decade or two, most homeowners had their houses rewired with 100-200 amps.

This chapter enables you to understand capacity as a function of physical, mental, and emotional nourishment, including areas of your life where you might not be getting enough of what you need to be great. The next two chapters give you specific, step-by-step ways to restore and increase capacity for your dreams, appetites and desires, and your mental capacity to "digest" the past and live in the present. Taken together, these three chapters give you the capacity to lead in your own life in ways that you may never have previously imagined. Take your time with this material; savor and digest it. It is quite a meal!

Nourishment: A Short Course

Having provided continuous nourishment for the child in her uterus, a mother gives the first and most primary form of nourishment to her child once she is born—her own milk. For this very reason, perhaps no issue is closer to women's hearts than the nourishment of children—not just their own, but everyone's. The chilling fact is that of the seven million people who die of hunger-related causes each year, the vast majority are children under five years of age, who die, not from starvation, but from chronic nutritional deficiencies that usually begin with their mothers who themselves are malnourished.

Startlingly, when you look into the condition of physical hunger, you also get a brilliant insight into the condition that women face spiritually and must overcome if they are to regain their place of power and effectiveness in human affairs.

When I use the word *spiritual* I do not mean *religious*. What I mean is that the spirit of women has been so malnourished by the dominator overlay that the very first requirement for women's leadership is to feed the spirit of what it is to be a woman, and to restore yourself to your full capacity. For that reason, it is useful to start with an overview of nourishment.

Every living thing needs sustenance. Humans are preprogrammed to crave nourishment. We need it to stay alive, grow, and perform all the functions of life. Food is not enough. Human beings need the nourishment of perceptual stimulation, physical and emotional contact, intellectual engagement, and a sense of the spirit of our humanity.

You can get large amounts of nourishment in one area and still be starved in another. A teacher I worked with had full permission to express her talents in her classroom, but no intimacy with her husband. Taking in more nourishment in one area to make up for what you are not getting in another area leads to a whole new set of problems. For example, buying new clothes does not make up for the deficiency you feel when you lack dreams and visions that are big enough for you to really stretch out and fly.

Even if you have nourishment available, if you do not have sufficient ability to absorb it, you will also have problems. An entrepreneur I know was overwhelmed in her business because she believed that the people who offered to help could not do what she needed as well as she could—an ancient trap. People who go it alone become chronically malnourished because they lose their capacity to absorb nourishment from others, an essential factor for human beings; we are clearly social animals.

Experts who study nutrition make four basic distinctions about nourishment. These distinctions are especially useful to people who are tackling the problem of physical hunger worldwide, but they also can be used to conceptualize nourishment in every area of our lives. Think of the distinctions as locations in the plus or minus universes. They are:

- Thriving or robustness (plus)
- Sufficiency (plus)
- Chronic malnutrition (minus)
- Starvation (minus)

The plus and minus universes are both states of being and states of mind. To bring this into focus, imagine that last month you reconciled your bank statement and discovered that your ending balance was –$1,000. You still had a few bills to pay. Life was tough at that moment. You wondered what mistake you made. You felt stupid. You may have even thought of yourself as "bad with money." This month you reconciled your statement and discovered that your balance was +$1,000. Life was good. You'd paid your bills and now you had something left over that you could use. You felt smart, maybe even more safe or secure.

What most people overlook in this story is that the amount, $1,000, was the same on each statement. In actual fact, it was not the amount but the "+" or "–" in front of the amount that made all the difference in your perception. What changed from one month to the next was the "universe" in which the $1,000 resided.

As in the "half-full, half-empty glass" analogy, not only does the universe in which your state of nourishment occurs give you different options, it also alters your personal perception and assessment of yourself as a human being.

The Plus Universe

Life in the plus universe of nourishment is good—really good. Life in the plus universe of nourishment is the land of appetite and desire. When most of us say, "I'm starved. I haven't eaten since early morning," it is only a colorful way of expressing our desire and appetite for food. If we had to, we could live off of the stored nutrients in our bodies for many days. Real hunger and starvation are an entirely different matter.

As with every universe, the plus universe of nourishment is not a single point or location. It covers a spectrum that begins at getting enough of what you need (sufficiency) and moves up to living abundantly (thriving). While no one in the plus universe suffers, the difference in how you feel if you are thriving versus living in sufficiency is dramatic, not only physically but mentally and emotionally as well. To live at full capacity is to thrive in all areas of life. To recognize your current location and to locate yourself consciously in the plus universe of nourishment, in every area of your life, is one of the most important ways you can empower yourself to get to the Promised Land of leadership and fulfillment.

In the plus universe, there is no driving force. There is only what you are "hankering for" and desires you want to fulfill. Rather than running after what you think you need, you begin to magnetize what you really want. True appetite has no desperation in it, so you are free to choose what you desire for the fun of it and to play with the people and circumstances that show up without any hidden agenda. People who live in the plus universe issue invitations, not orders. When you have enough of what you need, you can relax and enjoy the process of getting wherever you want to go. You can change your mind when you discover something you want more than what you desire now. Most importantly, you can add what other people desire to your own list. There is plenty for everyone in the plus universe, so you can help yourself to whatever looks good to you. The plus universe is where gratitude lives.

You might say that thriving is a state of mastery in the plus universe. It requires you to use fully what you have been given and stretch out in the game of desire, rather than playing it safe. To thrive is to acknowledge that there is no danger of living in the minus universe, so the worst thing that can happen if you take a chance and lose is that you will still be in a state of sufficiency.

About ten years ago, when I was still developing my thinking about fulfillment and leadership, I lived for a year with a couple who were friends of mine. One night the husband and I were sitting up in the hot tub and I told him I felt like a loser, because I wasn't doing as well as I thought I should. Kevin looked completely surprised and said, "Bill, you go for your dreams and take chances that I know I'm too afraid to take. That's what makes you a winner, not how much money you have or whether you're winning or losing at any given moment."

Many people, even wealthy people, are afraid that somehow they will lose everything and be living on the streets. It is a common fear in our culture and prevents playing for our full greatness. Several years ago, I had the startling revelation that no matter what happens financially, I have enough people who love me that I will never live on the streets and I will always have the basic necessities. As a matter of fact, when I went through a deep slump financially, a close friend invited me to live with her in her magnificent home. I was there for more than a year. When I realized that I could stop my internal dramas about basic survival, all that was left to do was to go wholeheartedly for my magnificence.

Thriving

You are thriving when you get more than enough of what you need to stay healthy, alert, and active. For example, where I live, many people eat "super foods" and supplements that are designed to increase vitality, activate more of the brain, and produce physical results that are not the norm. The people who use these products also tend to exercise, balance their diets carefully, and stay away from chemicals and drugs that suppress the body's natural vitality. They value optimum wellness. These are people with energy to burn and radiant health. Relatively few people in our culture of fast food and obesity live in a physical state of thriving, though we often praise it as a noble goal—especially for others.

People who are thriving are robust, exuding health and well-being. They are normally full-bodied, energetic, and dynamic. All the equipment is operating the way it should, and it shows. Their mental state is enthusiastic and spirited. We call them hearty, unafraid to enjoy their lives. They have a feeling of operating at peak while remaining in balance. They are a pleasure to be around, because they take pleasure in everything around them.

Sufficiency

You have sufficient nourishment when the muscles, glands, and organ systems of your body operate smoothly and efficiently. You have enough energy to last through the day and get things done. Your immune system works well and, although you may have occasional bouts of illness, for the most part you are healthy. When you have enough nourishment, you have the ability to focus and to absorb and process information in ways that are seen as appropriate. Mental, physical, and emotional processes are synchronized and you live your life against a background of wellness.

In developed countries, almost all people have sufficient access to food to meet the minimum requirements for health. They get enough nourishment to promote their vital processes and stay relatively healthy. Many countries require that foods have labels that tell you their nutritional value and government agencies that require sanitary standards to be met to insure the basic quality of food. If you do not have enough money to buy food, most developed countries have assistance programs that enable you to get the food you need.

Life in the plus universe of nourishment is stable. You have a platform that enables you to live your life day to day with an ease that most of us take for granted. To be thriving, you must stand on the platform of sufficiency first. What distinguishes thriving from sufficiency is a qualitative difference that may be best expressed by comparing ordinary people to Olympians. Olympians follow special regimens that support optimum performance. They are committed to the kind of physical results that are beyond the requirements for a good quality of life. As I heard one Olympics commentator say, "The winner of the gold in this race will win by tenths of a second. Every one of these athletes is extraordinary— the best of the best. The winner is the one who can reach just a little bit farther today than all the rest."

In the world we envision, where all people are able to lead productive lives, one of the necessary conditions is sufficiency of nourishment. For example, women who are malnourished give birth to children who are also malnourished. Early malnourishment often results in physical and mental conditions that put a cap on a child's ability to grow into a healthy and productive adult. People who have not developed adequately physically and mentally often require more attention and services than people who have had sufficient nourishment. Unless interrupted, the cycle continues from one generation to the next.

The Minus Universe

The minus universe of nourishment is the universe of problems, and it can keep you leading your life as if it were a constant set of problems to solve. Like the plus universe, it covers a spectrum, only this one starts at barely surviving and spirals down to starvation. In the real world of hunger, the minus universe starts with poverty and ends in death.

In the world of empowerment or spirit, the minus universe starts with never having quite enough or ignoring certain needs, and can end with the loss of the capacity to open to and enjoy areas of life that are essential for human beings. When you live in the minus universe of being human, you develop blind spots in your perception of your gifts and talents, the value you could have to others, and the quality of life you could have for yourself. Once you begin to recognize where you need to be nourished, you can begin a process of filling to sufficiency. Sufficiency is the starting point of the plus universe.

For two years I volunteered in Joan Holmes's office at The Hunger Project. I did things I did not necessarily think were important or crucial—addressing envelopes, running errands, and the like. One day while I was typing envelopes, I felt a big presence behind me. When I turned around, it was Joan. My first reaction was that I had done something wrong. Joan smiled at me and said, "Bill, I was just sitting at my desk and saw you here and I suddenly realized that without you I would never be able to do my job, so I wanted to thank you and let you know how much I appreciate you." I was speechless. I couldn't imagine why a women in her position would have noticed me.

Later that day, as I tried to tell my fiancée what had happened, I burst into tears. That may have been the very first time I had a clear experience that someone recognized my value apart from what I was doing. On that day I began a process of nourishing my sense of worth and visibility that has continued to this day. First there was the recognition of the blind spots; then there was the journey to sufficiency. Later on, thriving became available.

Chronic Malnutrition

The challenge with the third level of nourishment, chronic malnutrition, is that it is invisible to most people. It is a condition where you get some nourishment, but never enough. The best way to talk about it is to give an example. You are visiting a developing country. You have heard that many people in this country do not get enough to eat every day, though most people do eat every day and there is no starvation. You realize you have not actually seen people who look hungry and emaciated. One day you notice a beautiful little girl who appears to be about six years

old. On inquiring, you find out that the beautiful little girl is really ten years old, but because she chronically does not get enough
essential nourishment, her growth is stunted. If she were six, she
would be perfect. At ten, she breaks your heart. Her malnutrition
is invisible unless you know more than what a first glance provides.

That is what makes chronic malnutrition so insidious. It looks
as if the person is doing well when really she is not. Even her
death certificate will not say she died from the effects of chronic
hunger, but rather from some disease that would never kill a
healthy, well-nourished person.

When you are malnourished, you are simultaneously ravenous
for what you lack and lacking the ability to take in what you need.
Even when you get nourishment, you feel as if it will never be
enough. Malnourished people gorge and, because they have no
capacity for what they have taken in, throw it up. There is a kind
of desperation that goes with chronic malnourishment that permeates your thinking. You feel that you will never get enough and believe that you, yourself, are not enough. Malnourished people feel
justified doing whatever it takes to get nourishment. In fact, crime
is highest in areas where people are poor and do not get enough.

Many people who have sufficient material resources experience deep psychological poverty. Like physically malnourished
people, psychologically malnourished people also feel justified
doing whatever it takes to get nourishment. "Dog eat dog," "Nice
guys finish last," and "He who has the most toys wins" are, in my
opinion, all strategies of people whose malnourishment is primarily spiritual in nature. Gorging may take the form of buying more
of what you do not need, hoarding what you have for fear of losing it, or feeling upset when other people get something you want.
Greed, stinginess, and jealousy are the hallmarks of psychological
malnourishment and stunt the spirit of humanness. We describe
people like this as "small-minded."

In the minus universe, there is never enough to go around.
No matter how much there is, everything seems scarce. Chronic

psychological malnourishment is a torture because no matter how much you have or how much more you get, it will never be enough to satisfy you.

Starvation

The fourth level of nourishment (though it can hardly be called nourishment) is starvation. When people are starved they go into shock and stop feeling. The body shuts down, preparing to die. If you put food in front of a starving person, she does not have the energy or desire to pick it up. In a spiritual way of saying it, the soul has left the body, though the body itself may still be alive. It is a state of living death.

The people who die from hunger are the most confronting example of the chronic malnutrition and starvation that all of us live with in one area of our lives or another. The malnutrition of the Western, developed world, as Mother Teresa so poignantly stated, is a spiritual poverty. It is a mirror for the physical poverty and malnutrition of the developing world and is a good example that life really is connected and holographic. In other words, in a world where hunger is killing seven million children a year, you cannot escape it by closing yourself off to the condition or physically overeating or pretending it does not exist. The hunger is holographic in human beings. Whether it manifests physically or spiritually is less important than that it manifests in everyone in one way or another.

To recognize where you are nourished and where you are malnourished is the beginning of the ability to increase your capacity to thrive. It is also a way to take a leadership position in The Feminine Principle. When you demonstrate your willingness to make yourself a priority in a world that tells you that everyone else comes first, you let yourself think outside the dominator model that has oppressed billions of women. Until you nourish yourself, you have nothing extraordinary to offer. What would be extraordinary is millions of people pioneering and demonstrating real sufficiency and empowering others to have it, too.

Real Hunger

During my thirties and early forties, I made a habit of fasting once or twice a year. I really enjoyed giving my digestive system some time off, cleaning out my body, and losing any unwanted pounds. Dieting sounded like having a weight problem. People were in awe of the willpower it takes to fast. Spiritual people throughout the ages have done it. Fasting had cachet.

Normally, for the first three or four days, I felt hungry—what people who study nutrition call *appetite*, the desire to eat that if not fulfilled will cause no real harm to the body. After that, appetite disappeared. My practice was to keep fasting until I had appetite again—usually ten to fifteen days.

The very last fast I did went on for fifty days. It started out just like any other fast I had done, but after fifteen days, appetite had not returned. After twenty-five days, I felt light as a feather and the cries of amazement from friends were loud. At forty days, I had the eerie feeling that I was passing some mystical threshold. I have a distinct memory of watching people eat food and thinking it was disgusting. I would no more have thought of putting food in my mouth than trying to eat a rock. I was skin and bones.

By day fifty, the signal for real hunger—eat or die—went off in me. It was one of the most terrifying sensations I have ever experienced. I was ravenous, nearly insane for food. Having some understanding of the subject, I was acutely aware that if I did not eat right away, in a short time I would go into a state of starvation, with lasting damage. At the same time, my capacity for nourishment had shrunk to nearly zero.

I forced myself to take nourishment. A small piece of apple was torture, though I felt insatiably hungry. After a mouthful of broth, I felt full beyond endurance. It took more than a week just to be able to eat a whole piece of fruit. This was a very frightening experience—one I would never care to relive. Finally, after five weeks, I regained my full appetite and came back to life as I knew it.

Opening to nourishment when you have been chronically malnourished or even starved is very challenging. Starvation brings with it a state of apathy that shields you from the horrible pain you would otherwise experience as you shut down to die. When you open again, you feel the pain. When people come out of any kind of starvation, whether physical or mental or emotional, they often think something horrible has happened. They begin to feel again, and the first thing they feel is pain. In the fifteen years that I have been helping people to open to leadership in The Feminine Principle, even though I tell them over and over what to expect, from time to time I have been accused of doing something terrible to them when they start opening again, because the pain can be intense. Let's face it, if something were not painful, you would not have shut down around it to begin with.

On the other hand, people who have been chronically malnourished or starved have a tendency to gorge when they finally start getting what they want, often sending them into shock or forcing them to throw up food that the body has no capacity to handle. Malnourishment is such a ravenous condition that you begin to feel you will *never* get enough to be satisfied. There is the temptation to stuff yourself, causing severe discomfort and a whole new set of problems. The one and only solution to the problem of starvation or chronic malnutrition is to systematically build capacity for the things that are really missing.

If you have a pattern of "overeating" in one area of your life to make up for what you cannot have in another area, you must reopen the area of life you have shut, re-pattern your behavior, and learn to live in balance. As with most things in life—whether growing a baby or a business or your power or effectiveness— increasing your capacity is a progressive, holographic process. All the requirements in all areas must be met if there is to be real increase in capacity, because life is connected. People like to pretend that they can selectively choose the areas they will open and the ones they will keep closed. This is like deciding to have your blood flow only to your right arm, but not your left, or like telling your body that it should only digest protein, but not carbohydrates.

Every time you open an area that has been shut down or malnourished, you create a wave of opening that impacts every single part of you. The style in which you open makes all the difference in the quality of the result you achieve and even your willingness to keep opening.

A State of Nourishment Survey

It is important to make an assessment of your own state of nourishment, to see where you are starting. Here is a checklist of basic topics. It is not a test. There is no right or wrong answer. You do not have to show it to anyone, so give yourself permission to be as honest as you can. My recommendation is that if you are not sure which category you fit in, pick the one that feels closest to where you think you are. Also, feel free to skip a category or even add your own to make the checklist more appropriate to you.

First, select all the areas where you are thriving. Then select all the areas where you feel you get enough. Then, select all the ones where you feel you chronically do not get enough. Finally, select those areas that feel starved. It is best not to analyze or think too much about each topic, but to take your first reaction and mark "T" (thriving), "Su" (Sufficient), "M" (Malnourished), or "St" (Starved) before each one.

How Well Nourished Am I?

____Ability to receive	____Self-validation
____Ability to love myself	____Asking for what I want
____In my career	____Sexual satisfaction
____Presence/charisma	____Sense of stature
____Connection with spirit	____Success

____Sense of contributing

____Equality with men

____Generosity

____Quality of life

____Home environment

____Ability to influence others

____Sense of leadership

____Love

____Peace of mind

____Physical closeness with others

____Being powerful

____Salary

____Time for myself

____Degree of being turned on

____Having visions and goals

____Close friends

____Emotional freedom

____Fulfillment in family

____Happiness

____Health

____Sense of individuality

____Intellectual stimulation

____Having a like-minded community

____Money/prosperity

____Personal effectiveness

____Emotional intimacy

____Ability to relax

____Career opportunities

____Time off

____Visibility—feeling seen

____Vitality

____Freedom from mental chatter

If you are like most people who have taken this survey, you will find that you have:

> Thriving: 3 to 10 categories
>
> Sufficiency: 8 to 17 categories
>
> Chronic Malnutrition: 5 to 15 categories
>
> Starvation: 1 to 7 categories

The good news is that most people who have done this checklist get enough or are thriving in more than fifty percent of categories. On the down side, there are on average six to sixteen categories where people report they are not nourished in the way they would like to be, including being starved. If you have six categories of malnutrition or starvation, you are operating at 85 percent; if sixteen categories, 60 percent. Compare this to the idea that if your child does not get at least a grade of 70 percent in school, she fails—and you certainly want more for her than 70 percent.

Of course, most of these categories are not physical or precisely measured, because how you rate your satisfaction is an experience you have, not a thing. These categories are not exchangeable. They are the composite that makes you whole. Think, for example, how it would be …

- To make a lot of money, but have no intellectual stimulation.
- To be intellectually brilliant, but have no access to spirit.
- To live in a beautiful environment, but have no turn-on or intimacy.

That is life with holes in it, a common human experience. The goal is life at 100 percent—wholeness.

Most human beings live with a fictitious idea we have inherited from the war-based thinking models. We pretend that as long as we have the categories covered that are vital for our survival—money, place to live, etc.—we can forget the rest or do without them. Because of the dominator indoctrination, we even expect some areas to be broken, to never work. People give up trying to do anything about them and say defiantly, "That's just the way I am. Take it or leave it." Subject closed.

Many of the women and men with whom I have worked are exceedingly successful. They walk into a room and command attention. They are well dressed; they speak well, are well schooled, and well traveled. You would like them immediately and envy their lives; however, when you have intimate conversations with them, you discover that pieces of their lives are missing. Their souls often feel injured in ways that do not allow their full joy. Their dreams are compromised. They have no clear appreciation of their gifts and talents. They may be estranged from their families and expect that things will never change. Like the malnourished ten-year-old who looks like a healthy six-year-old, these people's malnutrition is invisible. In fact, in intimate conversations with them, I have had scores of successful women express despair that no one ever offered anything, because they were doing such a good job of covering up their need.

People make up for "this" with "that." They do not think that they will ever get an adequate helping of "this," so they better take twice as much "that." Regrettably, "this" does not replace "that" any more than carbohydrates replace protein. As in chronic malnutrition, everything looks great at first glance. The condition reveals itself only when you peer into it more deeply.

The Balance Point

You can gorge on what you don't need and never feel satisfied. When I first started bodybuilding in my early forties, I was a vegetarian. My trainer, Beth, a competitive bodybuilder, told me to eat a healthy meal after I finished my workout, in order to build muscle mass. I would go to the local burrito place and get a big veggie burrito. I ate and ate until my belly hurt and I thought I would explode, yet I still did not feel satisfied. When I complained, Beth said, "Bill, you are focusing on the wrong thing. After a workout like this, you need protein. When you get a vegetarian burrito, you get mostly carbohydrates. You have to eat a little chicken or fish or red meat; otherwise, you will always be hungry." After just a few ounces of fish, I would start feeling satisfied, though it was nothing I would have thought of myself.

To increase capacity you have to bring every area up to speed and expand from there, in the same way that you need every kind of nutrient to be healthy and thriving. What you really need to nourish yourself may or may not have anything to do with your opinions or beliefs about it. Fortunately, beliefs can be changed, though most people act as if they have no idea that they can change their minds (beliefs) anytime they want in favor of something that expands and fulfills them. It bears repeating: you are not stuck with any belief. Beliefs can and should be changed when they do not give you the pleasure of life.

If you are not getting everything you need, start by changing your belief system (model) before you do more of what already has not gotten you what you need.

You may also pay greater attention to the parts of your life that are working and still not achieve greater capacity. In my years of bodybuilding, I often noticed that young men worked incessantly on their chests and spent much less time on their legs. The result was a body that was out of proportion, with a gigantic chest and arms and spindly, underdeveloped legs. In bodybuilding, as in life, well-rounded looks, feels, and functions better.

Finally, building a state of real nutrition is a process that takes time. People join gyms to get in shape, work out strenuously for two or three days, and then are so sore that they get discouraged and quit. The same is true for people with hunger of all kinds. This phenomenon has been especially true of the human potential workshop crowd, who go to intensive weekends where they are blasted open emotionally, beyond their capacity to hold the opening, and wind up going back to the way they were in a week or two. Then they take the next workshop to open again and spend years "working on themselves" rather than building a sustainable capacity. As with any long-term venture, slow and steady leads to sustainable capacity.

Increasing Your Capacity

There are three conditions that can make all the difference in the way you build your capacity and your success with it. They are as necessary for you to win as light, water, and soil are for a plant to grow.

Start Where You Are

Here is an excerpt from a conversation I had with my friend, Jewel, a co-founder of The Women's Leadership Program, and a woman with an enormous capacity. We based our conversation on the information in the State of Nourishment Survey. "In my spiritual life, I need a sense of something bigger than myself to which I am connected, a way to communicate with my spirit, and the sense that life wants the best for me and I can trust it. I also want to experience my spirit as it comes through me as a woman, not in relationship to some male image of God. When I nourish myself with these elements, my spirit grows and develops.

"Mentally, I need creative ideas that open new vistas, a sense of the continual learning process of living, and intelligent people to get input from and to bounce ideas off. I crave conversations with people who have spiritual and emotional depth and are blazing new trails. Emotionally, I need to feel, but of all the feelings I need, the one that nourishes me most is love—every kind of love, including altruistic love. Physically, I need food, water, air, and exercise, but also to touch and be touched. I love feeling relaxed and excited at the same time, not necessarily about anything in particular, but just about being alive and enjoying the energy I feel.

"Sexually, I need enough pleasure frequently enough to be relaxed and open, turned on and living in my body. I also love feeling erotic and sensual. I love clothes that feel good, fragrances that are beautiful, and all manner of romantic accessories—candles, beautiful scarves, comfortable furniture, erotic literature, and massage. I also need intimacy—to feel and be felt—not only with a lover, but with family and friends, my child, and people who hold the same spiritual belief in the joy of life that I do.

"Professionally, I need career opportunities that challenge me to grow and be more skillful, professional relationships that stimulate me, and work that contributes something useful to the quality of life at large. Socially, I need family, lovers, friends, playmates, and acquaintances. Community is a must. I also require attention and personal acknowledgment from my community.

"I know that I need all these things in all these areas all the time if I want a great life. Life is not a trade-off—lots of sex, but no intimacy, or lots of thinking but no emotion, lots of work but no play. In my own view, a great life is not an accident; it takes careful and conscious managing, like anything of value and importance. I have to keep monitoring all these areas to make sure I'm not selling out.

"I don't always have everything in balance. Sometimes when I'm feeling especially out of sorts, I wake up, so to speak, and realize that I have not been nourishing some important areas of my life. When you live like this, you stop taking things for granted because you know that whatever you don't cultivate goes to seed in a hurry."

Jewel is at the far end of the spectrum of women who are leading in their knowledge of what they need and in their ability to get it. She has been developing her voice for her real needs for more than fifteen years, in what she refers to as an ongoing dialogue with herself and women friends who really know her.

To begin, it is very important to get a baseline measurement so you know where you stand right now. It certainly does not have to stay that way, but it is extremely hard to get where you are going if you do not know where you are. This can be challenging and bring up experiences and emotions that you might have carefully put away.

When you take the State of Nourishment Survey, you begin to get a clear picture of which areas are really nourished and which are not. Your judgments of how you got that way or what it means about you as a person are not really very important. What is important is to get turned on about having full nourishment and capacity in every area of your life.

Actually, you had very little to do with the models of belief that have systematically nourished or starved you. We live in a culture of trade-off—a success-based culture. It was here long before you ever appeared on the scene. We are taught that if you want this, you can't have that. It is called making your compromise with life. When I hear that someone has "settled down," more often than not I hear it as "settled for."

Congress believes deeply in compromise. Almost every bill that is passed is a compromise measure of some kind. In order for the people who proposed the bill to get it passed, they had to give up something else they really believed in. Sometimes they had to promise to support something they did not really believe in. Selling your soul for one thing to get another is the Devil's deal and is a standard practice of war- or success-based thinking. In medical terminology, when your body is compromised, it becomes sick. If too compromised, it dies. The spirit of our humanity is no different. Give up your heart and you lose your soul.

Put Yourself First

If you listen to the safety information provided by flight attendants as you are readying to take off, you know that airlines suggest putting your own oxygen mask on first and then putting on your children's. It makes sense. You are the one responsible for the safety of your children. If you put your children's masks on first and run out of oxygen yourself, who is left to take care of them?

If you do not give to yourself, you have nothing of value to give anyone. This is not some mystical advice. Even the battery in your car automatically recharges itself while your car runs. Everyone knows what happens when you leave the headlights on all night after you have turned the car off. By morning, the battery is dead. Human beings are no different.

To increase your capacity, you have to put yourself first. This violates what many women have been taught to think is the essence of The Feminine Principle. In actuality, this is only the dominator model talking and is the antithesis of The Feminine Principle, which values inclusivity. To put yourself first is an act

of feminine leadership that breaks the back of thousands of years
of cultural suppression of women's importance and worthiness. To
include yourself in the generosity that you normally are so willing
to give to others is the beginning of a New Feminine Principle,
free from the "starvation of self" that women have been taught
to expect as their lot in life. In a world where women are seen to
be second class or not to even exist as true human beings, women
have traditionally been allotted what is left over when everyone
else gets what they need. This is still true of food in many developing countries where women and girls eat last.

The African American community has a piece of wisdom that
addresses this directly: "When Mama's happy, everybody's happy."
Women have been taught and encouraged to be generous with the
people around them. You can count on that from most women.
When a woman puts herself first and fills up, she automatically
starts feeding the people around her. The generosity you experience as a woman is empowered, not suppressed, by putting yourself first and feeding yourself in the ways you need to be effective.
The point is that if you are going to nurture others, you have to
have something to nurture them with. If you are malnourished or
starved, you have nothing to give.

Go Step by Step

The only safe and sure way that I know of to increase capacity is to
enlarge it step by step. This is similar to the advice people who are
taking yoga classes receive. They are told to stretch to the limit of
their comfort and then relax into some small additional amount of
stretch. Even a quarter of an inch is fine. Over time, the additional
stretch becomes their new standard, enabling them to reach for
another small amount of stretch. That does not mean that breakthroughs or leaps cannot occur. They often do. It might even be
that the constant small gains are what facilitate the breakthrough.

Filling yourself when you have been malnourished has a life
and requirements of its own, no different from a child who is

developing in you. You cannot rush it without risking adverse effects, even considerable harm. In a world where we expect everything to be instantaneous, you might not like to hear this, but refilling takes whatever time it takes. To rush the natural processes that are built into you is to risk the quality and sustainability of the result. Having stated that caveat, there are also ways to encourage and maximize the process that are safe and pleasurable.

Trimtabs: Fine-Tuning Capacity

There is a device on the rudders of large ships called a trimtab (it's like a rudder on the rudder). This relatively modest-size device uses small amounts of leverage to move the ship's rudder, which in turn steers the ship. In other words, small movements of the trimtab have the power to set off, so to speak, a chain reaction that can move massive ships weighing thousands of tons.

Two of the most powerful and effective trimtabs for building capacity are ...

- Appetite and desire
- Completion

These trimtabs can move a huge mass of material in your life and get you going in the direction of full capacity safely and elegantly. The next two chapters show you how to use these powerful trimtabs to arrive at a new capacity with minimum stress and maximum enjoyment. Before you leave this chapter, it is a good idea to let go of the hallowed belief of the dominator model, "No pain, no gain." A few months ago I looked up this saying, which millions of people chant robotically day after day and make their reality. Much to my surprise, I found the quote ascribed to Benjamin Franklin, a personal hero of mine, who reportedly was a kind and gentle man. What Mr. Franklin actually said was, "Without pains, there is no gain." In his time, "pains" meant meticulous attention to detail, as in "she took pains to make sure that every person felt comfortable."

Please do take pains to understand and practice appetite and desire and completion, but forget pain and suffering. They are just not part of the equation and, belief to the contrary, really don't improve the result. Often, they are actually counterproductive and slow down the process of learning.

Nourishment and growth are part of the pleasure of The Feminine Principle. Take pleasure in learning to use the trimtabs. Have fun with them. You'll learn them more quickly if you do; and you will at the same time validate an essential aspect of The Feminine Principle, namely that the style is just as important as the result.

Chapter 5

Appetite and Desire (the First Trimtab)

It's difficult to imagine that a relatively small part of the rudder can turn an ocean liner that weighs thousands of tons, but that is exactly what trimtabs do. The Greek mathematician Archimedes clearly knew the value of trimtabs when he said, "Give me a lever and a place to stand and I will lift the earth." In the world of human leadership and empowerment, great leaders are living trimtabs who turn the course of humanity and create new futures by their visions. John Kennedy's trimtab remark to Congress that the United States should commit itself to having a man on the moon created the Space Age. Germaine Greer's *The Feminine Mystique* launched the modern women's movement. Anyone at any time can be a trimtab, not just the powerful and well known. One of my intentions for this book is to create millions of new leaders who become trimtabs wherever they are.

If you are like most human beings, though you might believe in miracles, you operate mostly in a plodding, pushing-forward style in your life. You'd like a miracle, but you really don't expect one. Flexing the muscle of your appetite and desire is a trimtab that can increase your capacity dramatically and rocket you forward in your life. When you combine high levels of turn-on with the willingness to tell the truth about what you really want, you call powerful forces into play that can change things dramatically in a short period of time. Chapter 5 explores this remarkable trimtab and shows you how to use one of your most powerful gifts—desire. In the world of feminine-style leadership, desire is everything.

Appetite and Desire Defined

You had lunch about an hour ago. While taking a walk and window shopping, you stop to admire a display of cakes in the window of a charming bakery. You really aren't hungry, but the display is so appealing, you decide to go into the shop. As you open the door, the smell of chocolate chip cookies fresh out of the oven makes you salivate. You can almost taste the hot, fresh cookies. Your stomach rumbles and all of a sudden you feel hungry.

Mentally or emotionally, that same kind of physical turn-on can be produced from a motivational talk, an advertisement, or a conversation with a friend. All of a sudden, you find yourself wanting to increase your business or make new career goals, start an exercise program, or study Italian in Florence. People talk about excellent presentations as having the power to "whet your appetite" or "make your mouth water" for whatever experience or product is being presented. The physical desire you feel, including strong emotion (which is always seated in powerful body sensations), attaches itself to an object and it/she/he takes on a magnetic quality as the object of your desire.

Appetite is object-related physical desire, *regardless of whether you act on it*. Did you buy the cookies in the bakery? Maybe. Maybe not. Appetite is desire for the sheer pleasure of it. And while it can spice up the game to treat a desired object as an "I must have it or I'll die" object, the reality is that you are really free to have it or not. Nothing "bad" will happen if you don't. A new car or a trip to Fiji is nothing you will die without. You can lust after an attractive person and not have to act on it. Though we speak about appetite in dramatic language, there really is no dinner "to die for." It's just that the feeling of desire is so strong it requires hyperbole.

Sometimes people forget that the desire originated in them, not in the object of their desire. They see the object of their desire as causative. In relationships, we often use the phrase, "*You* turn *me* on (or off)," but if you remember a night when you had no sexual desire, you will notice that almost nothing your partner could do had the power to turn you on. On another night, when you were bursting with desire, everything turned you on. The point is that it's your turn-on. You control the on/off switch in yourself.

Obsession is desire for which, if the object of desire is not available, there is no acceptable replacement of equal value. Additionally, the object of desire takes on the qualitative aspect of a need, and not attaining it is seen as life-threatening when it really is not. Hunger is a physical need, not a psychological obsession. Hunger is the experience of acute physical lack that forces you to find something to eat or face real consequences leading to death. There really is no acceptable substitute for food for someone who needs it to survive. With obsession, there is a *pretense* that there is no acceptable substitute for the object of the obsession. This is especially true in the culture of obsessive love that we glorify endlessly in our media. "You're my world and I can't live without you" is rarely true.

You could say that appetite operates in the world of "want" and hunger in the world of "need." Real needs for human beings are few: air, water, food, shelter, and connection (especially in the early years). Anything and everything else falls into the category of appetite or add-on or "give me some." Consider this last statement in light of the way we have been trained to feel that we absolutely need even the most superfluous consumer goods and services. To separate out what you really need from what you desire is a source of enormous power.

Objects of desire have real turn-on value because they originated from our physical turn-on. The turn-on motivates us to take action. Goals are made from the commitment to obtain an object of desire. Actions come out of commitment and goals. To take action to achieve a goal is natural when the goal is a turn-on for you. The goal magnetizes you rather than drives you.

You don't have to make any particular desire into a goal. You can express desire just for the fun of desiring. Many people take courses because they want a degree. Others take courses without

any degree in mind, just because they enjoy taking them. They
go to travelogue evenings, not because they intend to spend three
months in Africa, but because they desire the experience of going
while staying right where they are.

There are six enjoyable ways you can use appetite and desire to
build more capacity in the shortest time possible through your own
natural process of filling. Using these practices to increase appetite
and desire is a way to live your life outside the duty-driven ethic
in which we live. It also pioneers new ways to open your capacity
that are completely in harmony with the feminine principles of
relatedness, nourishment, growth, and the ultimate human goal of
happiness.

One: Practice Wanting

Nothing is more powerful or enjoyable than practicing wanting for
the sheer pleasure of it. When men shop, they are normally goal-
oriented. They get in, buy, and get out. Women, on the other hand,
enjoy browsing just for the pleasure of seeing what's available. You
can think of the practice of appetite and desire as internal window
shopping. Whether you "buy" or not is irrelevant.

To actively practice wanting involves one very important step
that takes you beyond mere window shopping: *practice speaking or
writing your appetites when you are turned on.* You will discover something very magical in the following experiment. First, make a list of
things you want when you are very turned on—exuberant, happy,
energized. Ask yourself, "What do I desire now?" You can use the
areas of life in the State of Nourishment Survey to guide your inquiry or come up with your own topics. Then compare that list to
what you would ordinarily desire.

You will discover that turn-on gives rise to a whole different list
than the list you make when you are not turned on. When you
are not turned on, duty rules. When you are, appetite and desire
triumph. The turn-on can come from many sources, such as reading, watching, or listening to someone or something that inspires

you; activities that revitalize you; emotional connection with other people; great sex; or deep meditative time. These are the moments when the pleasure centers of the body are most open and the desire you experience is untainted by fear or obligation or failure. Appetite, by its nature, needs to be free from coercion of any kind. If there is coercion, it is not appetite; it is obligation, with its associated feeling of "need."

Being turned on when you make lists of your appetites is the very best way to find out what you really desire—free from the "shoulds" that have been programmed into you. The great part about paying attention to what you want when you are turned on is that the turn-on is already built into the object of your desire. Imagine a time when something was so "juicy" for you to desire that every time you thought of it, you laughed or flushed or got "all fired up." The turn-on acts like jet fuel that moves you quickly where you want to go. You have more energy, so you get in gear more quickly to have your desire fulfilled. Increased turn-on sharpens your perceptual apparatus so you are more acutely aware and see new opportunities you might ordinarily miss. Turn-on gives you more of what the Jewish people call *chutzpah*, an ability to act audaciously. Increased turn-on also puts you in a state of excitement and happiness that makes everything easier and more fun while you're doing it. Turn-on is attractive; it turns up your voltage and lights you up so you are more visible. People see you as "hot" or "on fire." Most people love to be around this kind of turn-on. It makes others want to play your game, to cheer you on and help you in ways that they normally might not. A very successful woman I know says, "Desire creates the party; turn-on sends out the invitations."

Though it is never necessary to make a goal out of what you desire when you are turned on, when you do make it a goal, the turn-on you feel attracts you to the people, circumstances, and experiences that facilitate having your goals met. Contrast this to making ambitious commitments based on obligation and duty and then trying to get turned on to them. When you are not turned

on to your commitments, they become coercive and kill pleasure in
you. This coercive element is a hallmark of the dominator model.

Two: Start Where You Are

The oft-quoted Johann von Goethe—eighteenth-century poet,
dramatist, and philosopher—may have said it all when he advised,
"Whatever you can do or dream you can, begin it. Boldness has genius, power, and magic in it." Look over your State of Nourishment
Survey and pick some topics. Then, get yourself turned on and
energized and make a list of what you desire in these areas—
knowing that what you desire today can change tomorrow. If you
have suppressed your appetite and desire for a long time, you may
need to start with simply desiring more appetite and more desire in
that particular area. You can, for example, desire to be more turned
on, to be clearer about your appetites, to be a person who has big
appetite and desire, and so on.

Because life is connected and holographic, anywhere you start is
a good place. This is not linear. There is no particular place to get
to and there is no particular end point to the game of appetite and
desire. Just the opposite—the point is to keep growing your appetite and desire for the rest of your life.

If you have areas on your State of Nourishment Survey that are
malnourished or starved, as almost everyone does, it stands to reason that you won't have the capacity to have everything you desire
right away. Filling up will be a process.

Ever heard the expression "My cup runneth over"? Imagine that
you have a capacity that is the equivalent of a five-gallon bowl. You
start praying with all your heart for God to give you everything
God really desires to give you—more than you could ever imagine.
The next day, much to your surprise, your bowl starts filling. At
first, it feels wonderful. Then, having reached its five-gallon capacity, the bowl keeps filling and the contents start running down
the sides until you are ankle-deep, and still the bowl keeps filling.
Suddenly, you hear a voice saying, "You prayed for God to give you

everything that God wants to give you and that amounts to three thousand five hundred and five gallons." You face the problem of what to do with the three thousand five hundred gallons for which you have no capacity. Most people yell, "Stop, that's all I can handle!"

Although it is fine to have appetite for things that are beyond your current capacity, when you make goals for which you have no actual capacity, they are "pie in the sky." This is really part of the gorging phenomenon that occurs with hunger. To begin with, have the appetite and do not make it a goal. Think of it as goal window shopping.

It is often easier to start with appetites that actually have some possibility of occurring, whether you choose to make them goals or not. Each and every time you include a new or bigger desire that has some actual possibility of occurring, you automatically increase your capacity for appetite and your ability to desire in real and concrete ways. All by itself, expressing your appetites is a way to get a bigger "bowl," an expanded capacity. You can build more quickly a capacity for your dreams if you start with desiring what you can readily see having right now.

Dreams vs. Appetite

It is useful here to distinguish dreams from appetite. Think of dreams as fantasies you have without regard to whether they could possibly happen. Dreams are vitally important because they enrich the power people have to try on ideas, situations, and other points of view. As in the figure/background relationship in a picture, dreams are the background of life; appetites are the figure. Generally, dreams create the size of the "world" that people operate in, but are not necessarily the objects of desire themselves. Dreams can and should be fantastical, even impossible. They are nourishment for the soul. Long before we had air travel, human beings dreamed of flying. They had no real possibility of being able to make their dream come true. Thousands of people over the centuries tried hundreds of variations on wings and flying apparatuses that were dismal failures. Then, early in the twentieth century, two brothers cracked the code and what had been impossible became a reality.

Dream your dreams, but when it comes to claiming your appetites, have them be in some way possible, in order to increase your "real time" capacity; otherwise, you will find yourself in the realm of "wishes" rather than appetites. For example, you can dream of spending the rest of your life in an island paradise, but you can have appetite for moving to a beach town. You can dream about winning a lottery, but you can have appetite for asking for a raise.

This does not mean that you should stop dreaming. Quite the contrary! To be ultimately powerful, you can create what I call *appetite steps* where you desire the progression of your appetite into the fulfillment of your dreams. When you do that, a dream becomes a vision. Millions of people have created appetite steps in home ownership in order to fulfill the vision of their dream house. For example, you are living in an apartment, and it is very difficult to imagine yourself owning a 7,000-square-foot home on a hundred acres of land. You can hold the dream and enjoy it, but real appetite starts when you desire a home you have some chance of owning. So you begin by desiring the down payment for a starter house. You also desire more education or a home business that will give you additional income, and you desire to rework your budget to give you more savings. Then you desire selling your starter home in two to four years and using the appreciation and your increased income to move up in the real estate market. You imagine finding a great house that needs some work and upgrading it over five years and selling it for the combined appreciated and upgraded value. All of a sudden, your dream home goes from pie in the sky to real possibility.

In business, an effective business plan takes a dream, delineates the appetite steps that make it possible, and creates plans for realizing those goals in a timely manner. Banks will not generally give loans for dreams, but they will fund powerfully argued business plans that fulfill visions.

The Power of Visions

There is one amazing exception to this rule of bank loans. It is a dazzling example of The Feminine Principle in leadership and of the power of appetite, dreams, and vision.

In Bangladesh, there is a miraculous organization called the Grameen Bank that gives loans averaging $100 to some of the poorest people in the world, people who lack resources at a level that is unfathomable for us. Ninety-four percent of the people to whom the Grameen Bank lends money are women. For you or me, $100 would accomplish very little and hardly be worth the trouble of applying for. But for these (mostly) women—who have dreams, visions, appetite, and ambition—these loans are a miracle, maybe the very first time anyone has trusted them with such a large sum of money.

Since its modest beginning in 1983, the bank has jealously guarded six basic principles:

1. The bank would lend only to the poorest of the poor.
2. The bank would remain women-focused.
3. The loans would be without collateral or security.
4. The borrower, not the bank, would decide for what business the loan would be utilized.
5. The bank would help and support the borrower in succeeding.
6. Borrowers pay as much or as little interest as is needed to keep the bank self-sufficient and not dependent on grants.

From all reports, the women who receive them consider these loans sacred debts. They are tickets to self-sufficiency and are not taken lightly. What is nearly unbelievable from our Western point of view is that Grameen Bank has given 16 million loans since its inception (about a half-billion dollars predicted this year). Its customer loyalty is unparalleled.

To get a loan from the bank, you must have a group of five people who act as the support "collateral" for two of the members who are allowed to take out loans. This group anchors and stabilizes individual borrowers and makes success more attainable. This is a feminine way to operate. As borrowers successfully pay back their loans, they are encouraged to take bigger loans to finance bigger ventures, completely consistent with building a capacity for more and being able to hold it. In one village where the bank operates, a woman said that her first loan was $25 and that she was really scared when she took it. Now, she said, she is paying back a loan to continue to build her business, at $25 a week—an unimaginable sum for her a few years ago.

Ninety-four percent of the Grameen Bank is owned by the poorest people—the vast majority of whom are women—in Bangladesh. The Bank is committed to helping its members grow financially. Members, the poorest of the poor, now have $183 million in savings in the bank. Average household income in villages where Grameen Bank operates is 50 percent higher than in villages where it does not.

Grameen Bank outperforms all other banks in Bangladesh and most banks around the world. Though nowhere in its literature does the bank say this, when I read the bank's statistics and track record, it is clear to me that the appetite of the women who participate in Grameen Bank's program is enormous. It is also obvious that these women are some of the most turned-on, committed people on earth, who have cracked the code on their impossible dream to be self-sustaining.

Three: Be Generous with Your Desire

Unlike school, in the game of appetite and desire, every answer is the right answer, whether general or specific, simple or elaborate. For example, in the area of salary, you may simply desire a raise

and one more week of vacation. Or you could desire a raise with
a bonus based on performance, with a promise of a promotion in
one year and payment of your membership dues in a prestigious
business club, with the use of your company's apartment in New
York at least one week a year.

Don't just think about material things. Include experiences
you want, like feeling powerful or being able to say what you
want freely or standing up to people who disagree with you. If
you have been starved in your appetite for a long time, it is useful to include in your list of what you want, how you will feel
when you have it, where you will be when you get it, and even
who is with you. For example, in standing up to people who disagree with you, you might see yourself in a meeting of your local
school, holding the floor until you are finished saying what you
want to say, feeling heat in your face and energy surging through
you, your heart pumping strongly, and a sense of pride in yourself swelling your chest.

As you get good at this, add subcategories to your list—
desires for your family, for your church or neighborhood, your
community, or even your world. Every single thing that you desire, whether for yourself or others, is really your own desire
expressing and enlarging your capacity to have more. Just remember to start with yourself and move outward. To be generous
with your appetite and desire is a very good investment.

Four: Be Playful and Eliminate Obligation

Go through the list you got when you were very turned on and
be meticulous about deleting or altering any items that have any
duty or obligation in them. This is a great way to break that pattern. For example, in your sexuality, you notice that you have
appetite to have more romance with your partner, but you realize
that your desire has an obligation to take care of your partner,
rather than asking for something for yourself. You eliminate the
obligation and ask, "What do I want about romance that really

turns me on?" Then you discover that what you really want is for your partner to call you once a day and say, "I'm thinking about you," or you want to ask your partner for an evening of lovemaking that is all about you.

Keep in mind that you do not have to do anything about your appetite. You can have it just for the fun of having it, whether you mention it to your partner or not. Obviously, if you mention it, your chances of getting what you want are considerably increased.

Five: Share Your Appetite and Desire

Breaking the code of silence about what you want by telling others generates more voltage around your desires. When you activate your voice—the power to tell the truth about who you really are and what you really want—you increase your ability to generate new possibilities and establish yourself as an authentic leader in other people's eyes. You also empower the person with whom you speak to speak about her own desires by giving her a role model of how it looks in practice.

An additional benefit is that when a person hears your desires and experiences those desires as real and possible for you, they add mass and power to your desires. If you want to be really turned on, let many people know what you desire. If you want your desires to become realities, find people who will add mass to your desires by wanting them for you and encouraging you to go for them.

A few words of advice: tell your appetites to people who are receptive and turned on, not to closed or skeptical people. They can kill the turn-on. There is nothing worse than having someone pick apart or analyze your appetites. As with flavors of ice cream, the real answer to why you want a particular thing is simply because you have a hankering for it. More importantly, the point of telling another person your appetites is to increase the turn-on you feel and even spread it around, opening new possibilities for whomever you have told. Pick people who love to play the game of turn-on and you'll always win. Leave the tough nuts for somebody else.

Take some chances telling other people your appetites. There is a built-in, unexamined belief in close relationships that people should be able to read each other's minds and figure out what the other person wants. If you have appetites that are outside the scope of the relationship you currently enjoy with another person, the one and only way to let the other person know is to say so.

A woman I coached was passed over for a particular job in the accounting department of a large company. When she confronted her boss and said she was being treated unfairly, her boss was shocked. She replied that my client had never expressed any interest in that job. Because she had expressed the desire to have more time with her family and that particular job required some weekends, her boss presumed that she would not be interested, even though she was highly qualified.

There is a well-known story about a priest who faithfully attended one of his parishioners during the woman's last few years. Though he was not doing it for this reason, he expected that his parishioner, a woman of some means, would leave a bequest to her parish, though he felt too polite to bring it up. When the woman died, the priest discovered that she had left her estate to the Humane Society. Disappointed and bewildered, the priest sought the advice of a close friend, who happened to be a salesman. After finishing his tale of disappointment, the priest asked his friend if he had any explanation for what had happened. His friend thought for a moment and said, "I don't know how it is in religion, but in business it's always good advice to ask for the sale."

Pay attention to the other person's response when you tell her your appetites. Though no one likes to have their appetites met with indifference, the responses you get are immediate feedback that can be used powerfully. Not every appetite you have will land in the other person the same way it landed in you. It is useful to discover who are your most enthusiastic allies for certain desires or kinds of desire. For example, there are people who will be interested in everything you desire about money. Others won't be interested in money, but will be deeply interested in your desires for your community. Sharing your appetites also gives you immediate feedback about your own level of turn-on as you speak. If you are not communicating your turn-on for the appetite you are expressing, your chances of getting a great response are decreased. You can watch yourself speak about your appetites in a mirror and learn to project enthusiasm with your voice, body posture, and gestures.

Sometimes your appetite may bring up jealousy in the other person, and she may feel excluded from what you desire. The easiest way to include her is to let her know that you want that for her, too, or that you wish everyone could have that as well. The very best friends of your appetites are people whom you do not have to enroll. From the moment you mention your appetites, they are committed to them for you. These people are like gold and should be treated that way.

Six: Generate Goals That Give You More

There is an enormous amount of appetite and desire that is only for the enjoyment of the moment. You may desire to live abroad for a year while you are speaking with your customers in Europe, but that does not mean that you have to start planning a move. With appetite and desire it is always your choice.

Here are two distinct and practical ways I have found to generate goals from my appetite list that further increase my appetite and expand my capacity for having more.

Watch for Recurring Appetites

If you have appetite and desire for something that keeps recurring as you list what you want over several weeks, it is a good policy to stop and consider whether this is something that deserves to be made into a concrete goal. If you make it into a concrete goal, you can use the goal to generate more appetite and desire from the goal itself and even to generate other goals.

For example, a client of mine had a goal of buying a new house. Though she owned a nice home, when she did her appetite list she realized over several months that she wanted a house that represented a different lifestyle (appetite). She looked and looked with no luck (action). She did lists of what she wanted in a house (appetite). While she was doing her lists, she desired over and over to clean out a storage closet in her master bedroom (appetite). Finally, after two weeks and several appearances on her lists, she decided to clean the closet in question (goal). While she was cleaning it, she found an old shoebox filled with business cards and notes of all kinds. Going through the cards, she found the telephone number of a casual friend whom she had not seen in quite a while. She said she felt an almost overwhelming desire to connect, so she decided to call her (appetite/action). As the two women caught up, they made plans for lunch (goal). The acquaintance mentioned that she had gotten her real estate license. My client explained what she was looking for and mentioned her frustration finding it (appetite). Her friend asked if she would like her to do a search (appetite). Ten days later, her friend called and said she had found something worth looking at (result). You know the rest ....

Pay Attention to Sudden Desires

When I am making my lists of appetites and I get a clear, sudden, out-of-the-blue realization of something I want, I consider it seriously. I know that part of the malnourishment I have experienced has put limits on what I can desire and something out of the blue might represent a breakthrough in my capacity level.

For example, after I received my Master's degree, I worked for two years in my hometown and then reapplied to complete my doctorate. I was accepted and even offered an assistantship to pay my basic expenses. I flew down to Athens, Georgia, to look for an apartment and get my curriculum set up. At lunch with Dan, a professor who had become a personal friend, he said that it was

obvious to him that in the two years I had been away I had out-
grown the program I was in, and that I should consider not return-
ing. Though I had appetite to return to school, had made it my
goal, and was taking action on it, I was shocked to recognize the
truth of what he was saying and withdrew from my Ph.D. program
on the spot. Flying home, I began to ask "What now?" and suddenly I had a strong desire to move to California. (I had never been
there.) After a few weeks of serious consideration, I packed my car
and drove to San Francisco. Twenty-eight years later, I am still in
California and know that decision to move was one of the best I
have ever made.

Some of life's most extraordinary opportunities come as a bolt
out of the blue. To have enough capacity to take advantage of them
makes all the difference. To follow up on my story about Dan, I had
a friend in graduate school with whom I had lost touch. I searched
for years but could not find her. Every year or two, I would feel the
appetite to reconnect and would search fruitlessly. Then, one day
about six months ago, I felt the urge again, and this time I suddenly
remembered that Dan had been a mentor and good friend of hers.
If anyone might know how to find her, he would. After all these
years, he was still listed in the Athens phone book. I called and we
spoke for nearly two hours, catching up and reminiscing. It was
as if no time at all had passed. I had the opportunity to thank him
for changing the course of my life. He also knew how to find my
friend—another reunion. Two months later, his son e-mailed me
to let me know that Dan had died suddenly. Though shocked and
saddened, I was also enormously thankful that I had followed my
desire to find my friend; otherwise, I would have missed out on an
extraordinary reunion with a man who had made a huge impact on
my life and was a true friend to me.

Playing the Bigger Game

As your capacity grows, let the goals you make be an expression of
that growth. This is a natural progression of the way life evolves.

The goals you make at age eleven are entirely different in magnitude and scope from the ones you make at twenty-five. One way to drink from the fountain of youth is to express and enlarge your appetite all through life and make new goals all the way to the end.

If you really want a bigger life, have appetites and desires that are for something bigger than your own personal survival or your little corner of the world. Make goals that get you in the biggest game you can find. I know a businesswoman who is turned on by the idea of building houses for the poorest migrant workers. "I love my job. It puts me in the public eye," she said, "but now I'm using my position to enlist support for my larger vision from all the people with whom I come in contact." The larger the world of your appetite and desire and the larger the goals that come from it, the bigger the capacity you give yourself. The bigger your capacity, the more power you have to have some very exciting experiences. There is unimaginable opportunity in letting yourself play in the Olympics of your own life.

It has seemed to me that ten million women and men who are masterful with The New Feminine Principle could be trimtab enough that the whole quality of life for all humanity would change. Though a large number, ten million is only one sixth of one percent of the people who inhabit our world. I have huge appetite and desire for these ten million people and have been devoting myself to finding a way to have this happen for more than ten years—one of many reasons why I am writing this book.

I also know that, ultimately, if I do not reach the goal of ten million—which I arbitrarily made up, just as you would any goal—probably nothing horrible will happen to me personally. Based on the idea that life is connected and holographic, it is also a strong possibility that some other person or group may, in fact, come up with a more viable option or way into the future we want. This goal is simply something that turns me on, that I can desire with all my heart, and that gives me a huge game to play with my life. No one but I ever said I had to do this or even desire it. However, here are some of the benefits that this appetite and the goal I made from it have given me over the years, benefits that I know I wouldn't have gotten otherwise.

- A bigger sense of myself and what is possible for me
- An expanded vision that makes many of the ordinary problems of life trivial
- A commitment to my goal that has allowed me to grow and take chances that I ordinarily would have been afraid to take
- Association with other people who have extraordinary visions
- The power to become an original thinker; that is, someone who can think outside the box and generate new ideas
- Comfort with and enjoyment of an amazing variety of people who have dissimilar backgrounds from mine
- Tolerance. I know these 10 million people will be a diverse group and I'll have to find a way to welcome all of them.
- Vitality and openness that are unusual in a man my age
- A sense of leadership at a global level
- A love affair with my life that is totally outside of anything I ever predicted for myself

Make no mistake. I want my goal. I want the numbers to tally and for the trimtab effect to set in. On the other hand, the person I have become over the past ten years is definitely worth playing the game for, whether the goal is met or not. It is certainly important to play for your goals, but win or lose, the act of desiring and going for your goals in and of itself activates a power that has magnificent benefits.

Give up your notions of smallness. Let go of the idea that you couldn't possibly impact the whole world. Someone could. It could be you. Dream your dreams. Have your desires and give birth to the capacity that is the full expression of yourself. Nothing could be more feminine. Nothing could be more needed at this particular time.

Chapter 6

Completion (the Second Trimtab)

When it comes to models of reality, "as above, so below" refers to the principle that what you believe and continue to think (above) determines the reality you live in and the outcomes you get (below). When you know that belief creates reality, every time you change a belief you have the power to change your reality, even if only in some small way. This is godly power. Regardless of what you have been told or how much you have been threatened, you can change any belief any time you want. You are not stuck with beliefs and you need no one's permission but your own to change them.

Given the cultural mindset in which we live, most people use the tactic of fighting to change their attitudes, unaware that the more you fight something, the stronger it grows. When I was a kid, there was a woven finger toy that was fun to play with. You put one finger of each hand in each end of the woven tube and then tried to extract them by pulling harder. All you did was make the toy grip your fingers more tightly. The one and only way to get your fingers out was to stop fighting the toy, push your fingers together, and gently extract them.

Though it is difficult to admit, the fight against breast cancer, the war on drunk drivers, the battle against gang violence, and dozens of other issue-wars, have had little effect to stem the growth of these problems. Yet in the face of the obvious, the general advice is to redouble our efforts, somewhat like throwing two gallons of gasoline on a fire when one gallon of gasoline didn't do the trick. This is one of the brutal realities of dominator-based thinking and is a source of suffering for billions of people.

The Feminine Principle, on the other hand, values inclusion, nourishment, growth, and acknowledgment as fundamental processes of life. This, of course, is in harmony with the way our bodies process the food we eat and is, therefore, natural to human beings. The value of completion, the second trimtab, lies in altering mindsets by applying processes that are completely natural to every human being and that have already been proven effective for sustaining and growing every single person.

Completion gives you the opportunity to take *any* belief or experience you have ever had and digest it, just as you would food, storing what is nourishing and valuable to you and eliminating the rest.

To quote the lead character of the eponymous *Auntie Mame*, "Life's a banquet and most poor suckers are starving to death." What she meant was that most people live their lives avoiding everything that could challenge their narrow worldview. By doing so, they limit the vitality, nourishment, growth, and enrichment they could get from a wide variety of experiences. It's amazing that, as adults, we have perfect freedom to eat or not eat whatever food we choose, but in the area of our thinking, we accept minimal freedom to choose.

When you know that the human spirit is capable of the same kind of digestion that the human body enjoys, it is a lot easier to participate in the banquet of life and be vitalized by it. Charisma, the extraordinary vitality that marks leaders and draws people to them, exists in them in direct proportion to their willingness to eat "meals" of life experiences that provide a kind of "super-nutrition."

Distinguishing Between Complete and Finished

To be able to digest beliefs and experiences and use them to expand your capacity and vitality, it is necessary to understand the difference between *complete* and *finished*. Though these words are often used interchangeably, the difference in the origin and meaning of the two words is vast.

Complete comes from a root word that means "to fill up." It is a state of wholeness or having all the necessary parts. Without "complete nutrition," physical problems arise. *Complete* can also imply the fulfillment of a process that enables something new to happen, as in "She completed the coursework requirements for her doctorate and began to write her graduate thesis." The experience of being complete is a sense of fullness, like the satisfied feeling you get after a good meal.

Finished, on the other hand, comes from a root word that means "end." In the physical universe, all things end. Marriages end by death or divorce. People die. Jobs end. Your automobile and clothing wear out and you get rid of them. We speak of the end of an era. These are, of course, important milestones that should be acknowledged.

In The Feminine Principle, the quality of your life and the happiness you experience depend on being complete, not finished. The major topics of your life—namely health, wealth, relationships, finances, career, spirituality, family, sexuality, and sense of worth—which connect to one another to produce a great life, go on and on. Specific events or experiences in each area may end, but the area itself does not. You can close your checking account at one bank, but chances are you will still have a checking account at some bank.

Finished but Not Complete

People experience problems when they are finished with something before they are complete with it. For example, severely premature children finish their time in the womb too soon and the process of physical development is not complete. With modern technology, many of these children live, but have handicaps because the cycle of development was not complete when they were born.

Psychologically, the problem of "finished, but not complete," is illustrated in the following example. You and I are talking on the

phone and I say something that offends you. You say that you are
finished with this conversation and will never speak to me again
and hang up. The call and maybe our friendship are ended physically, but chances are neither one of us feels full and satisfied. Just
the opposite—our experience lives on as undigested material that
has the power to give us a mighty bellyache. For days, weeks, and
months each of us will go over the call, get upset again, make our
justifications, and stay right where we were when we ended the
call. This is finished, but not complete—a dead end. If your body
did that, you would be rushed to the hospital to have your stomach
pumped to remove the undigested food.

For most people, *complete* and *finished* are deeply confused and
smashed together. As a psychotherapist I saw dozens of clients who
were suffering because someone they were estranged from had died.
Many people live with the idea that they will never be able to move
on because they did not have a chance to finish. In reality, they
were finished, but they were not complete. When you acknowledge
all the parts or aspects of an experience, a function of the principle
of inclusion, you are complete and life begins to move along. The
completion process gives you the power to acknowledge all the
parts, taking in what is useful and eliminating the rest. Spiritual
"digestion" can have a completely miraculous effect on your life.

Complete but Not Finished

Now consider in the following example the principle "complete but
not finished." You just spent four or five hours out in your garden
pulling weeds, pruning plants, and watering. Even as you enter
your house and kick your mud boots off, you imagine you hear the
next weed popping up. You smile. You know you will never be finished gardening—an idea you love because you love to garden. At
the same time, you feel complete, that is, full and satisfied with gardening at this moment. People call this happiness. Because *complete*
also implies the fulfillment of a process that allows something new

to happen, you shift gears and take a bath, have dinner, and so on. This is "complete, but not finished," a great way to go through life.

Individual companies come and go, but business goes on. Individuals come and go, but family goes on. Neighbors come and go, but neighborhood goes on. No one is really finished until they die, but you can be complete—full and satisfied at any moment.

Consider the sexual joy you have when you are in love. You are filled up by it. It radiates out from both of you. It is the very energy that creates your deeper intimacy, your children, and your sense of connection and belonging with another. Contrast that with the puritanical notion that when you have finished making children, sex naturally dies. Medical authorities are finally acknowledging that sexual activity is the best single thing you can do all the way through life to remain vital and lucid. It is difficult to think of any other activity that has so much feeling of being complete (full and satisfied) imbedded in it.

Hobbies like collecting art, comic books, seashells, foreign coins, autographs, and pictures of Elvis, have no particular end point in sight. Puttering may be the closest that adults ever get to the kind of play kids enjoy nearly every minute. Play, at its best, is not goal-oriented, competitive behavior. It is done for the intrinsic pleasure it provides and the creations it gives birth to. Frankly, if your life is not about the pleasure of being alive, just what is the point of it?

People who practice dance and meditation are not "practicing to get it right," but rather deepening their experience and mastery of their chosen discipline. The mastery of life lies in maintaining it at increasingly higher levels of participation and interest, pioneering new ways to enjoy it at every stage, and celebrating how good it is to be alive for these few short years that we are given. To be complete, but not finished, lets you live life in present time and be available for whatever life has to offer. This is one definition of agelessness.

Being Complete

When I was a psychotherapist, I often had the experience that people were carrying around the weight of the world on their shoulders. Old hurts from childhood and incomplete relationships or experiences had them lugging around so much baggage from the past that they hardly had any freedom to enjoy the present. These incompletions seemed to have lives of their own. If life is indeed a banquet with thousands of experiences to choose from and be nourished by, these people had no ability to digest what they had taken in, get fueled by it, and move on.

The point is that not everything life dishes out is epicurean, but even the most unappealing "dish" can be digested and the value extracted from it. Then you are free to pick something you would enjoy more.

Completion is a straightforward process, a tool you can use to digest any belief or experience you have had, so you can use it to have greater capacity to take advantage of whatever life makes available to you. This process is based on two things:

1. How you report on a meal you have eaten.
2. How your body digests what you have eaten.

The Completion Process

Take any belief you hold or any experience you have had—for example, leadership, my job, being a woman, the neighborhood where I grew up, my level of education, my first marriage. Fix the topic in your mind and answer the following questions in the most concise way you can. List whatever answers you'd like until you are satisfied that you have said what you wanted to say. There are no right or wrong answers. If you want to, you may write out your list, but this isn't necessary.

1. **About this topic, what have I gotten of value that I must say to be complete?**

   List all the things that have been valuable or pleasurable or useful, and feel yourself absorbing them as nourishment.

   If the topic you are completing is intrinsically negative—for example, violence you suffered, being fired, and the like—simply acknowledge that the relief you feel in completing this topic is the one and only pleasure. When you have been deeply in pain, relief is nearly orgasmic, like the pleasure you feel after getting rid of a toothache.

2. **About this topic, what has not been valuable that I must say to be complete?**

   Make your list. When you are complete, eliminate this information, just the way your body does with waste or toxic material. Mentally throw away your list. You can also visualize a computer deleting the file containing this information. If you've written your list, tear it up. Feel the relief.

3. **About this topic, who do I need to apologize to and for what in order to be complete?**

   Be specific: I apologize to myself for criticizing myself so much. I apologize to my best friend (employee, husband, coworker, or whomever) for taking out my frustration on them. I apologize to the people (name them) to whom I have not expressed thanks for their help. I apologize to (name them) for my judgments about them.

   Feel the power of your apology run through you to make things right. Then delete the file and feel the relief of letting it go.

   For the completion process to work it is not necessary to call or write people and apologize to them directly, though I have done it many times with wonderful results. Many people find it powerful to feel themselves sending the energy of their apology to everyone to whom they have apologized. This is a wonderful and generous emotional pleasure.

4. **About this topic, who do I need to thank and for what in order to be complete?**

   If you believe in God, start by thanking God. Be specific. Then thank yourself and be specific. Then thank everyone else specifically for the part they played regarding this topic. Be generous with your thanks and praise. It is absolutely unnecessary to actually contact anyone to thank them personally for the process to work. It is generous to send the energy of your gratitude to everyone you have mentioned with an intention that right at this moment they are being blessed. Feel the power of gratitude run through you. It is one of life's greatest pleasures. Then eliminate or delete the list from your conscious attention. This is the same thing you do when you make a list of thank-you notes you need to write for birthday presents you received. You cross off each name as you finish writing their note, until finally your list is finished and you toss the piece of paper with all the names in the wastebasket.

5. **About this topic, what else do I need to say to be complete?**

   If there is something you forgot to say in one of the other steps, whether it is a big deal or something miniscule, say it. Then eliminate or delete the list.

   Sometimes what people leave out are the feelings they have. For example, "I'm so sad that I've carried this belief with me for so many years and held on to it," or "I can finally admit how delightful that chapter of my life was." Simply feel the emotions you have regarding a completion and then let them go. There's nothing else to do with them.

6. **Make this declaration: "Regarding this topic, I am complete, up to date. I have taken in the nourishment and eliminated the rest. I am grateful."**

   The trick is to make the declaration and move on. The power of declaration is miraculous in that it is an act of consciously changing course. Although it is wonderful to remember your pleasures from time to time, don't keep going over the information in the completion process. If you have written out the completion list, throw away your notes. Every time you go over your notes, you will inadvertently activate that information again.

After you have done a completion process, you have updated your consciousness—cleaning your mental house or reorganizing your files. You are left with a packet of pleasurable information with which to nourish yourself over and over, just as you do with physical nourishment stored in your body's tissues. You will have also deleted all the rest of the information that was taking up room in your consciousness.

Moving On

We live with a belief in our culture that to be complete with the past is arduous work requiring years of counseling, insight, or simply emotional struggle. This belief is an artifact of the dominator culture where struggle is a way of life. In actual fact, the past does not even exist except as a function of the conversations you have in your head about it. When you order those conversations, extract the value from them, acknowledge what went wrong, and clean them up in your own head, the past loses its grip.

In a training I attended, there was a woman who spent her life arguing with her deceased parents about what they had or had not done that had ruined her life. The facilitator asked her how old her parents were when they had her and she reported that they were both twenty-one years old when she was born. Then the facilitator asked all the people in the training who were in their early twenties to stand up, and she picked a woman and a man. When the facilitator interviewed the young woman and man about their lives, it was obvious that they were just starting out, were completely naïve about what it would take to be parents, and were in many ways babes in the woods themselves.

The facilitator turned to the woman and said, "This is who you've been arguing with for nearly sixty years?" The woman, who looked stunned, finally said, "I always thought parents should be mature and know everything. I guess my parents were just a couple of kids trying to figure out what to do with this kid they had created."

You can do mentally what the body already knows how to do physically. As you do more completions, you clean up your "personal operating file" by storing what has been valuable and deleting old, damaging, or unuseful information. In the process you rewire your perceptual filters to put special emphasis on what is valuable. That value will be more readily accessible to you because you have reconditioned yourself to pay attention to it and you have less clutter to sort through to get to it. In a world where people almost always notice and make important what is wrong, noticing the value first gives you a power to use what you have to your best advantage. In The Feminine Principle, nourishment is one of the central pleasures of life, one that facilitates health and growth. Take the nourishment that is available and flush the rest away.

How to Complete Anything in Twelve Minutes or Less

In seminars I have conducted over the years, I have encouraged people to be complete with the whole history of their lives in twelve minutes or less. Impossible, you say? Only if you live in a world where everything should and must take a long time. In the early nineteenth century, crossing from Europe to America could take a few months. A hundred years later, it had shortened to a few weeks. Now it takes a few hours.

It is not only advances in technology that have allowed for swifter passage. Behind every one of those breakthroughs in technology was a shift in the belief in what is possible. Someone's dream and desire activated appetite steps, goals, and actions that have materialized in "fasten your seatbelts for takeoff."

Having done personal completions with hundreds of people, I have discovered that what takes time is not the actual information of the completion process, but the stories people tell. Many people have a propensity to give long, complicated examples of items on their completion list. The story becomes more important than the completion itself, and I have even seen people forget they were doing a completion process as they got lost in the story they were telling. It is enormously powerful—and an economy of time—to list the items and leave out the stories, fascinating though they may be.

1. Choose a topic, such as your life to date, leadership, career, capacity, finances, spirituality, sexuality, or any other thing you want to bring up-to-date.

2. Divide the completion process into the following segments: four minutes for the nourishment category, two minutes for the pain and suffering category (now that's a switch!), two minutes for apology, three minutes for thanks, and one minute for anything else, including your declaration that you are complete. Twelve minutes flat!

3. Now, set a timer and make yourself stick to it. If you are finished with a category before the time is up, move on. If you are still caught up in a category when the time is up, move on and save whatever is left over for the miscellaneous category at the end. Deadlines empower us to get things done and not drag them out. When you get to the point, leave out your stories, drop the drama, and move on, you develop more clarity and focus, two very useful tools for leaders.

When you have mastered the twelve-minute completion, you can set a goal to do the process in ten minutes. When you have mastered that, try eight minutes, and so on until you have mastered the art of doing completions in a few minutes. The trick is to get to the heart of what you have to say without endlessly embellishing and repeating, a common trap that is the downside of the way women learn to communicate.

The key ingredient for doing completions is the clear intention to be complete, not getting it perfect. You do not have to get every single word or category right to be complete.

A Sample Completion

You could tell scores of stories and give hundreds of examples to illustrate your life. In fact, people spend hundreds of hours and thousands of dollars talking about their lives so they can have some freedom from the past. Sometimes it works; often it doesn't. Following is a sample completion on your personal history. Please do not worry about how this will affect your life. Your life will not be over; it will simply be complete, up to the moment. When you complete a topic, you update yourself and you start living more fully in the present. This gives you the power to make things better, because you can only change the present, not the past. (Even your memories of the past occur in present time.)

You can still choose to relate to your life in any way you desire. It's just that you will have a brand-new freedom about it; it's not linked to baggage from the past.

Topic: My Personal History (My Life to Date)

1. **List what is valuable (4 minutes).**

   For example: My family/ancestry and the neighborhood I grew up in. My education. The friends I made along the way. The places I've lived. My Faith. Lovers/marital partner(s). Mentors. My children. My career(s). The way I've lived. My health. Experiences I've had. Celebrations, particular trips, or important events. Periods of my life that were important to me.

   - Add your own unique items to the list.
   - Absorb the value from your list and nourish yourself.

2. **List what is not valuable (2 minutes).**

   For example: Fears of all kinds. The rigid values of my parents/church/culture. Ideas about myself, the world, religion, money, or sex that have limited me. Compromises I have made. Doing things I hated to please others. Guilt, heartbreak, useless anger, or worry. Chances I took or did not take that did not turn out well. Injuries/illnesses. Jobs I've held that were not right for me. Love affairs gone wrong. Losses of people or important things.

- Add your own unique items to the list.
- Delete the list and feel relieved.

3. Apologize (2 minutes).

For example, for any ways that you have blamed your parents for how you are now as an adult. For criticizing yourself. For any judgments you have about yourself or others that have limited you. For any grudges you bear. For important or damaging mistakes you have made with yourself or others.

- Add your own unique items.
- Send your apology spiritually to the people you have mentioned, delete the list, and feel relieved.

4. Give thanks (3 minutes).

For example, God for your life and for where you are now. Your parents for giving you life and the members of your family for doing the best they could or for any acts of personal kindness that you especially remember. Yourself for whatever great choices you have made. Important mentors, role models, teachers, lovers, and friends. People who were important along the way.

- Add your own unique items.
- Send the energy of your thanks as a blessing to those you mentioned, then delete the list and feel relieved.

5. Say anything else you need to say to be complete (1 minute).

For example, special memories or sentiments that must be expressed. Leftover judgments you carry about the past. Any feelings that are left over from the past. Things you forgot to say in the previous steps.

- Add your own unique items.
- Delete the list and feel relieved.

6. Declare.

"Regarding my personal history, I am complete, up-to-date. I have taken in the nourishment that was available and eliminated the rest. I am grateful."

A New World

If you want to take a huge leap forward and change your life, take thirty-six minutes and do this experiment. Do separate completions on your life, on being a woman (man), and on your leadership to date. (You can use the previous completion for your personal history.) Over the next few hours/days, notice how your perceptions change. Feel how your emotional responses change. Pay attention to the changes in your body sensations. Notice what gets freed up in you. Like people coming from the Old Country to the New World, it is useful to take what is valuable, leave the rest behind, and get whatever else you need when you arrive.

If you are like most people who have tried this experiment, you will recognize a new sense of relaxation in your body, a release of emotional pressure, and a quieting of your mind. Now multiply that by the number of completions you could do on various beliefs and experiences you have had, and you will begin to appreciate the kind of expanded capacity and freedom that is available to you.

Though it might seem like a staggering number to you right now, when I had done the completion process about two thousand times over a couple of years on various topics, something startling happened. It was as if the chain that kept me shackled to the belief that my models of reality are true snapped. I knew I would never be held captive again by any particular model of belief. I also knew that I have the power to alter my belief systems anytime I want at will, enabling me to enlarge my capacity and make room for more of what I really want. When I discovered that I have the power to alter my reality anytime I want, I cried with happiness.

How and When to Use the Completion Process

Use the completion process on any belief, experience, or topic you want to digest, no matter how recently or long ago it occurred. It is important to complete how the experience or belief landed in you, not the "facts" or what you think someone else thinks. As you know, your view depends on which side of the airplane you are sitting.

Get to the heart of the matter in each category and say what is necessary to be complete with as little storytelling as possible. There are two very good reasons for saying what you have to say quickly and moving on. First, if you are like most people, you have already spent too much time and energy on the topic. Second, if you spend a lot of time on each topic, you will feel overwhelmed. Then completions will become another work item, rather than a way to get your freedom easily.

When at all possible, say the topic of your completions in ways that acknowledge what you already have. My colleague Deborah Kelley and I were talking about what would make the completion process better. She said, "You know, it seems that when people start out with this process, they tend to focus on problems that they want to get rid of, and by focusing on them, they make them more important. It would be far better if everyone did the completion process as a way to magnetize the world they want to live in."

I asked her what that meant in practice. She said, "It is better to affirm and celebrate what you already have that is right and then expand to have more, than to keep focusing on what you think is wrong. For example, rather than doing a completion on a health problem you have, it would be better to do it on the current level of your health. Rather than how you feel stuck, the current level of freedom you enjoy. Rather than lack of faith in yourself, your current level of self-confidence."

If you are reading this book, you have enough health, personal freedom, and self-confidence that you are not locked away or at death's door. One ounce of what you have is better than all the oceans of what you do not have, because when you acknowledge what you already have, it locates you "on the board," that is, in the plus universe of the "haves" rather than in the minus universe of "have-nots." When you are on the board, you are in a world where expansion of what you have and greater capacity for what you want are possible.

Use the completion process at major "finishing" milestones such as your birthday, New Year's Eve, or your wedding anniversary; when you leave a job, home, town, or relationship; and after a death, the end of a project, or even a trip or vacation. These are great opportunities to summarize and bring everything up to date.

Do at least one completion each and every day. You can do the completion process in the in-between time you have during the day. This includes when you are taking a shower or bath, waiting in line or in traffic or for an appointment, taking off your makeup, getting ready for bed, or waiting to fall asleep at night. Do a completion on the day you have had, while you are waiting to fall asleep, and wake up the next morning brand new.

For many years, I have made it my practice to do a completion after every meeting during the day and at the end of the day so I sleep peacefully. It takes only a few minutes to update and fully nourish myself. This is the same principle as doing smaller loads of laundry regularly, rather than waiting till you have laundry piled up and nothing clean to wear.

The Power of "Connected and Holographic" in Completions

Right after I had formulated the completion process, a friend of mine, Carole, invited me to facilitate a six-month course for top producers in the large and very successful real estate office she managed. I asked for a volunteer to show the class how powerful this process is. The volunteer would be asked to do a completion on a topic that was so important that to digest it would be to start a new chapter of life.

A talented, intelligent, and lovely woman named Cindy raised her hand. She explained that four years before, her husband had simply disappeared. She had checked everywhere—hospitals, police, credit card companies, anywhere she could think of. No one could find him. He had vanished, leaving her and their young son in grief, with a mystery that might never be solved. She was thinking of having her husband declared legally dead. For all she knew, he was. She was at a loss for what else she could do. Needless to say, this incompletion was draining the vitality out of her life.

I explained the completion process and asked her what she wanted to digest. As with most people who have a problem, Cindy wanted to start with the disappearance. Instead, following Deborah Kelley's advice, I asked her to do the process on the entire relationship, including falling in love and getting married, having her child, and so on—not just the disappearance itself. In other words, I wanted Cindy to be complete with the whole thing, not just the upset, so she would have the freedom to move on and create more relationship.

I had not yet invented the twelve-minute game, so the process took quite a while. During the completion process Cindy began to remember the wonderful times she and her husband had, not just the heartbreak of his disappearance. She was moved when she remembered the whole relationship, not just one part of it. She apologized for keeping her life on hold and even forgave him for disappearing. She expressed her gratitude for their relationship and for the beautiful son he had made with her. Because of the depth of the emotion she was feeling, the process took almost an hour.

Finally, Cindy declared that she was complete. She looked radiant—beautiful color in her cheeks, happy and relieved inside, relaxed, her mind still and clear. She looked and felt like a different person. Everyone who witnessed her completion process was amazed that she could go from heartbroken to peaceful and happy in such a short time; after all, an hour in comparison to four years is a miniscule amount of time. It certainly did defy conventional logic about how much time it takes to change.

A month later, at our next meeting, Cindy returned with an almost unbelievable follow-up story. She told us that four days after she did the process, out of the blue her husband called. It was Mother's Day. She was stunned. He said that the marriage and his responsibilities were overwhelming him, so he ran off, knowing she would take care of their child. He said that somehow he knew it was all right to call now. This is the amazing power of The Feminine Principle's cornerstone that life is connected and holographic.

A year later, I saw Cindy at a holiday party. She said that she had gotten a divorce and had found a wonderful man with whom to share her life, and that what had happened was a thing of the past. (This is a perfect example of the meaning of *complete* that implies the fulfillment of a process, which enables you to naturally move on.)

Though Cindy's result with the completion process was one of the most remarkable I have witnessed, there are literally thousands of other miraculous stories, big and small, that have resulted from doing this process, including a woman who was able to complete her relationship with her sexually abusive father and move on.

Old, painful memories disappear, new people appear, and opportunities open when you have room for them. It is extremely difficult to take in new kinds of nourishment when you have not digested what you already have. Even a gourmet meal, if it sits in your stomach too long, will cause a bellyache and leave you unable to take in more nourishment. Completions take you out of the dead end of "finished, but not complete" and enable you to be whole every moment you are alive—complete, but not finished. These two states of being are as different as Kansas and Oz.

You Are in Charge

You have in your hands now two of the most powerful tools I know—appetite and desire, and the completion process—for ending the malnutrition that resulted from overlaying the dominator cultural view onto The Feminine Principle. Appetite and desire have the power to open your dreams, enlarge your sense of what you can have, and feed the future you really want. Completion has the power to store what you value, eliminate what is not useful or even toxic, and reorient your entire perception to nourishment, which you have the power to claim anytime you want.

It is so feminine to plan a big meal, have it be beautiful and delicious, and feel the satisfaction of great dining with good friends. In those moments, you celebrate life and life itself renews and enlarges itself in you.

You have the power to lead in your own unique way by planning the banquet of your own life and enjoying it down to the very last forkful. You have the power to lead by inspiring people to gather at your "table," whether at work, at home, or in community, by demonstrating your remarkable capacity for life and by teaching them to be complete in every moment. (I have had women teach the completion process to their elementary school classes and their own young children.)

You have the power to empower other women and men by leading the way in using every experience in life for your benefit. You have the power to stop playing the victim, and you have the power to help others stop, too.

Let's face it. Most of life is really good. It seems preposterous to keep focusing on what is missing when you are inundated with more of the good life than people in any other culture in the entire history of the world. You have more freedom, more education, more health, more material things—including indoor plumbing, air conditioning, heating, food, and clothing—than most kings and queens ever had. You are an elevated being in comparison with the billions of people who have already lived. To focus on and enlarge your incredible good fortune is an act of leadership in The Feminine Principle that forges a brand-new perspective for human beings.

Maybe most importantly, you have the power to change the macrocosmic reality we share that puts our very future in jeopardy. You can change this reality by changing the microcosmic reality in which you live. By nourishing yourself, expressing your appetite and desire, and opening into leadership in your own life, you will speak to the world around you and magnetize the world to your desire.

Chapter 7

The Key of Truth

The last three chapters, taken together, were an exploration of the key of capacity—what it is, how to develop it, and its necessity for establishing a New Feminine Principle. In this chapter, we will explore the key of truth, in particular how you can recognize your own personal truth and find the freedom that you will need to lead your life with magnificence and empower the magnificence of others.

We are all familiar with the term "the glass ceiling." Though you can see the level where you would like to be, there is a transparent barrier that doesn't allow you to get there. This chapter is not about rebelling against that barrier or even smashing through it. It is about making the glass ceiling disappear. The key of truth is the power to "relocate" to another universe of perception where the barrier ceases to exist and you have the freedom to claim the life you want. The key of truth is your ticket to that universe.

In a speech to celebrate International Women's Day this year, Joan Holmes said that women are the key to healthier societies, to faster economic growth, and to greater social justice. They are the key to the future. As you will see in this chapter, when you tell the truth that sets you free, you discover that you have the power and freedom to be a first-class human being. The ability to choose freely—especially in the face of circumstances or pressure to the contrary—is an essential ingredient of being a leader. To choose to live a first-class life in the face of nearly a whole world that disagrees with you by dint of thousands of years of culture and tradition establishes a whole new definition of what it is to be a global leader. Of that kind of leadership, a whole new future is born.

The Problem of Being Second Class

If you ever have had the pleasure of flying first class on an extended flight, you know that first class is not just the front of the plane. It is a completely different world from coach, which is second class, though no airline personnel would ever say so. The essential thing you pay more for in first class is not the food, the free drinks, or the service, though they are good. In first class, you have a lot more space. Depending on the size of the airplane, you can stretch out all the way, sometimes even convert your seat into a bed. Space is an ultimate luxury, as the millions of people who live in Hong Kong, New York, and Tokyo know.

People who can afford to fly first class regularly have in the background of their thinking a model of entitlement in which they expect certain standards of service, beauty, or respect. Now, suppose you called your airline to book a first-class ticket and were told they only had two left and were saving them in case someone better than you called. Suppose, like Rosa Parks, you faced this when you tried to get on a bus and sit in the front (first class). Suppose, like nightclubs in Manhattan and Los Angeles, there were velvet ropes that opened instantly for some privileged people while you stood in line with almost no chance of getting in. Finally, suppose your money could not buy you some things, no matter how much you had or how much you tried.

This is the world of second class, of less than, of being overlooked for no apparent reason, of responding rather than being responded to. This is a world that women know intimately. It is a world where you spend your life wanting the best for everyone around you with no freedom to put yourself first and to expect the very things you want for others.

The Glass Ceiling

"We knew that they had let the drawbridge down for us and we scurried across it into the male club called business school, but that doesn't mean we knew what to do when we got there." So states a woman who has an MBA from the Wharton School of Business, one of the most renowned business schools in the world, regarding her admission to that institution in the early 1970s. "This was a time when prestigious schools were scrambling to find women to meet the requirements of opening their schools out beyond the white, male population. When I met the admissions director, he told me that with my background in economics, if I made application to the school, I was in. Just like that.

"I was in a program with less than twenty other women, in a school that had hundreds of men. Was I second class?" She repeated my question. "I can tell you this. In one of my classes I sat down next to a male student who looked at me and said, 'What are you doing here, looking for a husband?'

"I have mixed feelings about getting my MBA. It was so clearly a 'male' thing to do. I took a job at what is now Citibank. It was a time when the movie *Annie Hall* was popular, so it was easy for us to start dressing like men. It was important not to be too feminine. Though the people at Citibank might have had the best intentions to open the doors of the Old Boys' Club, it felt as if we were on probation, with the men waiting to see if we could measure up to them. Looking back, there was definitely a glass ceiling, though I was in no danger of hitting it in my first few years there. I remember something vividly, a manager who grew up in Queens. He did not have an MBA and resented like hell the idea of me, a woman with my MBA from Wharton, coming in on the fast track. He made life so miserable for me, I finally asked for a transfer."

The woman who gave this interview is a Tony-nominated Broadway producer. She has written and produced a feature film and is a published author. She also helped to launch a brand-new broadcasting product for the stock market, which created a sizeable return on her work investment. At the end of the interview she suggested, "Maybe you should talk to women who are younger than me. It's probably different for them."

I took her advice and interviewed a woman who is an executive with one of the largest national waste management companies. At forty, she is doing well—an innovator in her company, a mover and shaker in the business community, and a leader in her church. We talked about women's leadership. "I was at our company's national executive convention last month. When I looked around, my estimate was less than 10 percent women at the meetings. I know at my table, I was the one and only woman executive. I also know that my company is working on diversity and wants to help women leaders."

Thirty-five years after the woman from Wharton started her studies, institutions and companies are still wanting and trying to help women come into leadership positions, often without much success. According to a report by The Annenberg Public Policy Center, the number of women executives in top communications companies—a field that would seem natural for women—is just 15 percent. "Men still hold the vast majority of [top management] positions," said former FCC commissioner Susan Ness. "The glass ceiling is firmly in place."

The Equal Pay Act has been on the books since 1963. The amount of pay all minorities make compared with white men is between 70–80 percent. Women make 77 percent of what men make, and it is predicted that this disparity will not disappear worldwide until 2050—two generations from now. (For women in the United States, parity will come sometime in the decade between 2040 and 2050.)

In *The Old Girls' Network* (Basic Books, Cambridge, MA, 2003), authors Sharon Whiteley, Kathy Elliott, and Connie Duckworth come right to the point. "Women who start businesses have the same motivation as men: self-actualization, personal achievement, and autonomy. So why is there a need for a book by women for women? ... Because of our cultural societal upbringing, we still don't feel entitled to succeed, to compete and win. ... Because there is a misconception that women don't have the characteristics needed to run an enterprise—the passion, the vision, the inherent skill set."

Logically, it makes no sense that genders of the human species could be seen as anything less than complementary, full and equal partners. Unfortunately, logic has nothing to do with humanity, though we like to pretend it does. There is a clear message in the dominator model of The Masculine Principle that women's leadership, intelligence, and power is at best second class and has no intrinsic right to be asserted outside the home.

The Cold Hard Facts About Being Second Class

Consider that in more than a few developing countries, the rate of abortion of female fetuses is significantly higher than males. In developing countries, girls have traditionally been the last ones to be fed in a household. They receive less health care and less education than their male counterparts. Girls and women are subjected to rigid controls of dress, behavior, and personal freedom, based on religious or cultural codes. Women have been mutilated in almost unimaginable ways, including foot binding and genital mutilation.

There are no accurate statistics on the number of women killed as witches, but witch hunts went on for three centuries and might have killed up to several million women. The systematic persecution of women of power was one of the ways that the male, priestly caste of Christianity ultimately gained power. Women who were targeted were often the healers or wise women of their communities or simply women who would not readily yield to the power of the priests (*The Burning Times* video documentary, 1990, Wellspring Media).

Women in so-called advanced societies, though better off in many ways than their sisters in the developing world, are often afraid to dine or travel or shop or walk alone, day or night, without fear of attack or verbal harassment. In conversations with hundreds of women, I have come to realize that the rights and privileges I take for granted as a man are denied to women. The right to say what I want, including "no" to what I do not want, to go out at night, to take a hike in the woods by myself, to sleep in my own bed and feel safe, to travel alone to other countries and feel that same way, does not exist for many, if not most, of the world's women and girls. As you know if you are a woman, the possibility of attack at any moment is a powerful ward against exploring your world too fully, even if nothing happens. Women and men not only live in completely different worlds of thinking, but they also live in radically different worlds of basic human freedoms.

As a white person, it is hard to imagine the subtle and not so subtle indignities that people of color put up with every single day. As a member of the Brahmin caste, it is beyond imagining what it means in real, practical terms to be "untouchable." In the world of men, it is equally difficult to consider what women are made to tolerate or forced to ignore as they go through the common, everyday experiences that make up their lives.

It is urgent to realize that although the dominator culture holds the belief that women are second class, women themselves, having internalized the belief, also believe they are second class. As a woman, whether you have worked on this issue personally or not, it is the automatic, emotional default setting to which the culture at large is tuned and to which you must continually respond.

My mentor and friend Joan Holmes, whom I have already mentioned, is one of the most brilliant, intelligent, and powerful women on earth. In addition to her duties as president of The Hunger Project, she is also a member of the council that works directly with the secretary general of the United Nations on viable solutions to the world's most pressing problems, especially poverty.

Joan said that in thinking through the beliefs that keep hunger in place, she recognized that, "in the world's eyes, my own personal pathology is my gender." She said that this realization was almost more than she could bear, because there was absolutely nothing that she or billions of other females could do about it. Citing her own mindset as an example, Joan said, "In 1977, when The Hunger Project was launched, I tentatively raised my hand and said I would manage it for three months. Inside, I was thinking, "Until they find a man who can run it.""

Though I stated it in Chapter 2, this bears repeating: Your mindset, which remains for the most part invisible and unexamined, is the background against which your life is shaped and played out. To examine your cultural "legacy" and change it from the inside out is one form of genius—something that Joan Holmes and women like her have been doing to discover a way through to the future we want.

To make visible in yourself what has previously been invisible to you is to take your life into your own hands and grant entitlements to yourself that otherwise would go unclaimed. Authentic leadership in this area shows up as the systematic dismantling of the model of "women are less than" that lives in women themselves. This is definitely a more difficult row to hoe than blaming the powers that be or other people. It is also a way of pioneering leadership and real empowerment. Before you can lobby for change in the world around you, you have to make the change in yourself. In Mahatma Gandhi's famous words, "(You) be the change you want in the world."

First Class

Since the dawn of the information age, power has not resided in more muscle, but in inventing new mindsets, bringing to consciousness what has been transparent, and rethinking the actual way we think. To rethink yourself as a first-class person is challenging, to say the least.

In discussions I have had over the years with thousands of women, many women take exception to the idea that they are not first class and, truthfully, some women had elevated themselves into first-class thinking long before I ever showed up. At the same time, the vast majority of women living in the world today demonstrate by their automatic behaviors the very problem we are facing as a world community. For example, in dozens of intense, intimate conversations over the years, I have been amazed to find that women will automatically stop what they are doing and pay full attention to any man who walks into the room. For their part, men feel free to interrupt women's conversations, because when you are first class, you do not have to consider those who are not. When a man and a woman begin to speak simultaneously, the woman will normally apologize and let the man speak first. Many people would say that these behaviors indicate a high degree of relationship and generosity on the part of women. My own experience tells me that, for the most part, these behaviors are not actively chosen but rather are automatic.

I certainly have no real idea what women experience by being born into a culture of second class; however, having been born into a blue-collar culture, I can say that it took several years to retrain myself from a working-class to an upper-middle-class point of view. For example, when I moved away from Philadelphia for the first time, a highly educated woman I met said that she thought I had a foreign accent and could barely understand me. I was shocked. I didn't even know I had an accent. For two years I worked on softening the hard nasal accent with which I grew up. I learned the verbal inflections and key vocabulary words of upper-middle-class people. There were literally hundreds of behaviors and points of view that I learned to recognize and incorporate. Absolutely none of this makes white-collar people better than blue-collar people; it does, however, create signals that people who are upper middle class recognize. In other words, I consciously learned a new social model—one that opened doors that were previously closed to me.

As a woman, when you wake up to the ways in which you allow yourself to act and to be treated as second class, it can be a profound shock, similar to the one I experienced when I discovered my accent. To systematically complete these old ways of seeing yourself is the first step. The second step is to voice first class in yourself in ways that transform your thinking and alter your response to the world around you. To find a voice for and tell the truth about who you really are, including your particular kind of genius, what you want (and don't want), and what you are committed to unleashes a whole new spirit of your humanity.

It is obvious that the idea of what is feminine and what is masculine can be examined, elevated, and reformulated anytime we choose. The place to start is with how The Feminine and Masculine Principles live in you, then to decide who you are in the matter of being feminine, and to reformulate the models you use any way you choose that gives you more of yourself. This includes traditionally masculine attributes that give you more of what you want.

Recent brain research has established the "plasticity" of the human brain, which is very good news. What this means is that men can be retrained to think emotionally, use more of their brains, and reorganize data in a more holographic portrayal of reality. It also means for women that they can be retrained to use power and command and to voice what they have not voiced before.

At the core of the ability to retrain people to exhibit new thinking and behavior are the mindsets that keep their old thinking and behavior in place. Without changing them, retraining is virtually impossible. When we finally get rid of the suppression of the dominator model on our ideas of masculine and feminine, what could easily occur is the full expression of humanity that lives in us all. To do that, it is necessary to start by telling the truth.

The Truth Will Set You Free

If you are a woman, you know that the shortest distance between two points might not be a straight line. It may be a quantum leap. Like science fiction writers, the prophets of our age, you may discover "worm holes," shortcuts in space/time that enable you to enter from one side of the galaxy and emerge on the other. Like magicians, you may discover that things really can disappear and something entirely new can show up to take their place—when you know the trick.

One of the most powerful "tricks" I know is one I did not invent. Buddha and Jesus were doing this trick millennia ago. They referred to it as telling the truth, and they said that it has the power to set you free. Like Buddha or Jesus or even Harry Houdini, the great magician and escape artist, you can learn to tell the truth and be set free. This is not some metaphysical mumbo-jumbo. You can learn the trick from a completely practical point of view, though the two great masters I have mentioned might have had a more cosmic Truth in mind when they spoke about it.

It is important to distinguish "telling the truth" from "being honest." Telling the truth is about identifying the thoughts, emotions, and physical experiences that have the power to free you to choose what is in your best interest. When people say they are being honest, they are more often expressing what is on their mind at the moment. For example, someone could say, "I'm telling the truth when I say that I hate my mother." It may be honestly how she feels at that moment. Whether it sets her free is a completely different story, as I learned as a psychotherapist listening to people express negative emotions about their parents over and over again without any significant change or improvement. It's fine to be honest. It's a quantum leap to tell the truth.

If you want to have competence in the practical art of telling the truth, throw away all your preconceptions about what the truth is. To save you some time, you will not find the truth in the jumble of religious, metaphysical, political, intellectual, psychological, or philosophical belief systems that have been sold wholesale to humanity and reinforced with fear and coercion. Beliefs about the truth are not the same as telling the truth. Also, give up your idea that the truth is some monolithic thing that, once found, applies to everyone in every case.

Instead, pay attention to what happens when you make a statement. If the result is that you are set free, then you are telling the truth. How do you know if you are set free? First, you need to discover what freedom is and how it manifests for human beings in real, observable, completely describable terms.

What Freedom Is

Let's start by looking into the definition of *freedom*. Freedom is "the power to act, think, or speak without the imposition of restraint." There are two important parts to this definition:

1. Freedom is a power.
2. Freedom is also an ability to choose without restraint (coercion).

Power is the first hallmark of freedom. To be a leader, you must have the ability and capacity for freedom. To develop a larger "bowl" to hold your appetites and desires is a source of power, because it gives you the capacity you need to lead in your own life and often hold the lives of others in your embrace. Power is also electricity, current, or as the engineers say, juice. To open your desire and feel the actual physical current that runs through you and to increase that current deliberately and enlarge your capacity for it are potent sources of power.

Choice is the second defining aspect of freedom. Freedom to choose resides in the realm of pure appetite because there is no need. Freedom is a hallmark of appetite, a pure "give me some." If you have real hunger for something, meaning you need it or you will have dire consequences, you have no freedom at all. Whatever you need, you must choose; therefore, need is always coercive.

Patrick Henry's ringing call to freedom, "Give me liberty or give me death," has inspired and empowered millions of Americans with its pure freedom to choose and pure appetite with no need even to stay alive. Pure inspiration!

The Experience of Freedom

Once you are clear about the definition of freedom, you can begin to craft the actual *experience* of freedom. To discover the experience of freedom, do the following simple exercise.

Imagine yourself at a time and place in your life when you experienced freedom. It could have been as simple as choosing what flavor of ice cream you wanted or how you were going to spend a free afternoon. Most people have thousands of these situational experiences of freedom over the course of a lifetime, so it is not as if we don't know what freedom is. Put yourself fully in the experience and feel again how you did then. Enjoy it. Feel the power of your choice. Next, pick another memory of freedom to choose and put yourself in it. Then, pick a third, fourth, or fifth memory and do the same thing. You will discover that the experience of freedom remains virtually the same regardless of the situation.

Having the same biological wiring as every other human being, you will discover three things when you experience freedom. The first thing is that emotionally you are happy. The second thing is that you are more alive—more energized—physically, while at the same time being relaxed. We associate more energy in the body with more tension, but that condition is only the case when you have no real freedom to choose. When you have choice, the energy is a current in a body that is relaxed and pliable. The third thing you will notice is that your mind is clear and quiet and alert. For this last experience alone, people meditate for years. You can have it without years of meditation.

Human experience occurs in three ways: emotionally, physically, and mentally. If you define the experience of the freedom to choose as the experience of being happy, energized, and relaxed, and mentally clear, quiet, and alert—all at the same time—you give yourself the key to unlock "The truth will set you free."

The trick is to use only the data that simultaneously gives you the emotional, physical, and mental experience of freedom. This is a very practical way to identify the truth—to take it out of the realm of the ephemeral and put it squarely in the realm of your body and your immediate experience.

How to Create Entitlement

Having defined freedom in ways that make it accessible—as an experience you already know—it is also useful to define entitlement for the same purpose. Entitlement is *to bestow a rank of nobility, rank, honor or dignity upon* and *to give (one) the right to do or have something; allow; qualify.* In the world of consensual agreement, leaders lead because someone has conferred the rank or the right to lead upon them. In a world where women are presumed to be second class, the opportunity for this bestowal of nobility (greatness and magnanimity), dignity (inherent worth), and the right (something due anyone by law, tradition or nature) is not automatic for women.

Fortunately, there is a way to bestow entitlement on yourself that no one has the power to revoke, by getting to the core of what is True in you and learning to do that in every situation. There are three essential ingredients necessary to access the truth in any situation, so that you have happiness, energy in a relaxed physical state, and mental clarity all occurring at the same time.

The Truth Must Be About You

The moment you say that your truth is about someone else, you become his or her victim. Victims have absolutely no freedom. Here is a pattern sexual partners sometimes use. First, they attribute their sexual desire to the other person, as in "*you* turn me on." Then, when they do not feel turned on, they attribute their lack of sexual desire to the other person, as in "*you* don't turn me on." Let's face it. On a day when you are really available sexually, anything your partner says or does has the power to turn you on. Conversely, when you are not really available sexually, almost nothing your partner says or does has the power to turn you on.

You are the only one who can empower your turn-on because only you have the power to determine in your body and your emotions and your mind when you are having the experiences that, taken together, are the experience of turn-on. The same holds true for determining what sets you free. You make the choice, and choosing is powerful.

Werner Erhard, the founder of *est* Training, the controversial program that launched the human potential seminar business in the United States, said, "The truth believed is a lie." What he meant is that when you believe someone else's truth, without having the actual living, personal experience of it yourself, it is a lie because it is only a belief. To have your own personal experience of what sets you free is the only truth there is.

The Truth Is Better Than You Think

Consider the general tone of the automatic voice that talks to you in your head. You would never speak to another person the way that voice speaks to you. The amount of cruelty people visit on themselves in the language they use to describe themselves is nearly sadistic.

No one really knows where the voice comes from, but it certainly is not pleasant or useful. Listen to that voice for a minute or two and you will discover that nothing it is saying to you will ever be the truth. The very best thing you can do with that voice is to ignore it (or disconnect it by doing completions on what it is saying). It stands to reason, then, that when you tell the truth, it will be much, much better than anything the automatic voice in your head is saying. That is why the truth is better than what you automatically think.

Though I have joked about it sometimes and said the voice is like an automatic public service announcement for unhappiness, it is no wonder that we are a people for whom depression is the number-one mental illness and antidepressants are among the leading prescription drugs. The voice most people hear in their heads is enough to make anyone depressed.

Several years ago when my late mother turned eighty, I felt a strong desire to try to explain my work to her. She knew I had been a therapist, but I had not shared with her the larger concerns and visions for my life. "You know, Mom," I said, "that voice that talks to you all the time and criticizes you and accuses you and puts you down?" She immediately and emphatically answered, "Yes." "Well," I said, "my vision is that if enough people were to tell the truth and live lives of happiness, that voice would disappear and a new voice that is kind and supportive and nurturing would emerge as a kind of new consciousness for human beings. That's what I'm working to accomplish." Her eyes got big and very clear and she said, "You really think you could do that?" This bright woman, who had been born in an entirely different era, had never traveled, and had finished only elementary school, knew exactly what I was talking about. I know that you do, too. You have the power to change that automatic voice by interrupting it and telling the truth.

The Truth Is Something You Have Never Voiced Before

This last condition is so obvious that it makes me laugh. When you tell the truth it sets you free. If you are stuck in any area of your life, then anything you have said previously cannot possibly be the truth, because if it were, you would be free. The only thing left to do with information that does not set you free is delete it, because no matter how much you go over it, it still will not set you free. To start deleting what the automatic voice in your head says to you by doing completions could save you thousands of hours of mental aggravation over the course of your lifetime—not to mention help you feel a lot more relaxed.

Something you have not voiced before comes as a bolt out of the blue, an "aha," a personal realization, an epiphany. You cannot get the truth by thinking harder any more than you can re-member someone's name by concentrating harder and harder on it. When you relax (one of the hallmarks of the truth), all of a sudden the name comes through. The truth is just like that.

Opening yourself and giving birth to a brand-new way of think-ing are the only ways you can get to the truth. Opening and giving birth are, fortunately, completely feminine principles.

One of the sources of power is the ability to take ideas and structure them in real, everyday experiences that you can have per-sonally. Though I have been speaking of entitlement specifically as the right to be first class, you can also define entitlement as your right to experience things firsthand and find your own truth about them. In a group I recently joined, there was an opinion that one of the members was unfriendly, even intimidating. I decided to put that opinion to the test. In the second meeting I attended, I smiled and sat down next to the member in question. He and I struck up an animated conversation and have since become good friends. Though you may trust another person's opinion, it is always best to make up your own mind.

How to Tell the Truth in Every Area of Your Life

If we wanted to, we could program a computer to list all the women who live in Florida. To be more specific, we could program for all the women in Florida who are over thirty-five. Then, all the women in Florida over thirty-five who are married. Then, all the women in Florida over thirty-five, married, who make more than $100,000, and who have more than three children. Theoretically, we could keep adding variable after variable until we narrowed down the field to one woman out of all the millions of women who live in Florida.

When you learn to identify the truth, you are taking all the pos-sible answers to the question "What is the truth about this subject?"

and sorting through them until you arrive at the answer that is all about you, better than you think, and nothing you have voiced before and that gives you the simultaneous experience of freedom mentally, emotionally, and physically. You may need to keep sorting through the possible answers a few, several, or many times before you get the exact answer that matches these criteria. No answer is intrinsically right or wrong. The only "right" answer is the one that satisfies all the criteria at the same time.

Learning to think this way is the beginning of discernment, a quality that is highly valued among leaders and skillful people of all kinds. More often than not, the true answer is not available among the choices you can readily think of and requires you to invent a whole new kind of answer that sets you free. When you train yourself to invent whole new kinds of answers, you become an original thinker, someone who thinks outside the box of the common reality and can play with new ideas for the sheer pleasure of it. The world we all want that will be a pleasure for us all will be invented by original thinkers.

To learn to tell the truth, first pick an area of importance to you. In the following example, I will use entitlement because it is an area of such overwhelming importance to women.

Dump out everything you have said to yourself so far about entitlement that has not set you free. (This is a major relief.) For example, imagine you have said you are entitled, but it has been only a reaction to not being entitled, and it has not made you feel any different. (Reacting by saying the equal and opposite seldom works because it is in opposition to something and therefore is forced or coerced.) You might have also said that people who think they are better than others are jerks. Or you might have said that you don't have enough education, were born into the wrong family, or are not strong enough to get entitlement. After saying these things, you notice that none of them gives you the experience of freedom. Just the opposite, they make you feel heavy and stuck. Delete this information. It will never be the truth.

Then, start your inquiry by asking "What can I say about entitlement that is only about me, that is better than anything I've been automatically thinking, that I have not voiced before, and that will set me free when I say it?" Remember that the experience of freedom is being emotionally happy, physically energized and relaxed, and mentally clear, alert, and quiet.

Let yourself play with your answers. There is no right answer, simply the answer that gives you the biggest experience of freedom. Open yourself to something you have never said before coming through you. It does not have to be logical; it just has to give you the experience of freedom. Now imagine you start to laugh when you hear inside you "To hell with entitlement, I'm a force of nature and I'll damned well take what I want." Lighter, freer, though there is an edge of anger in it.

You sit with the question a little while longer and open yourself to something that would give you even more freedom. Out of the blue, you remember holding your newborn child in your arms and suddenly you hear "Life is a gift. I don't have to earn it. All I have to do is accept and enjoy my own life, just as I'm enjoying my baby's life." You melt. You are moved. You feel yourself relaxing and surges of energy go through your body. All of a sudden, your mind, which usually goes a mile a minute, stops. All the hallmarks are there at the same time. You are in the presence of the truth. It is a holy state because you are whole and complete, everything connected at that moment. Now imagine starting to live your life in that truth; you have the possibility of a completely different life from one of duty, fear, inferiority, or working harder and harder.

If life is a gift and you are already alive, no one has to give it to you and no one can take it away. If it came with the territory when you were born, you can use your life any way you want. "Life is a gift. I don't have to earn it. All I have to do is accept it" has a whole lot more freedom in it than "I've got to prove myself," "Only the strong survive," "Men are better than women," or "I'll show them."

Your truth is your truth. Your best friend's truth that sets her free might be something entirely different, because the truth is a personal invention, not a dogma to be evangelized—though it is wonderful to share it with others in the same way you would your appetite and desire, to increase your turn-on and theirs.

Finally, if you never got exactly what the truth is, but you played with saying things that gave you more freedom all the time, you would also hit the jackpot. The point of telling the truth as a long-term practice is that it magnetizes your thinking to what is more elevating, enlivening, and empowering. Consider altering and shaping your speaking so that every time you speak to yourself or anyone else, you take the energy up and give everyone more freedom to operate. That is empowerment at the highest level.

Try this. Say the following phrases to yourself and decide for yourself which ones give you more freedom:

- I'm going to have to fight my way to the top.
- I am whole, perfect, complete, and connected.
- My parents and the culture I was raised in are responsible for my problems.
- I am a gift to the people around me.
- My connection to myself is the most important thing I could have.
- Having a relationship is what defines me.
- Everyone can be right.
- This area of my life is permanently broken.
- I am invisible.
- I am juicy.
- I am mediocre.
- I am one of a kind.

Listen to what you are saying about yourself or your world—not just the big things but everything you say as you go through your day. If whatever you are saying gives you more emotional joy, physical energy, relaxation, and mental clarity, claim it for your own and use it to set yourself free. If it doesn't turn you on or if it weighs you down, dump it and don't give it another thought. It will never be the truth.

First-Class and Bad to the Bone

I have a friend named Beth who is an extraordinary bodybuilder. Beth has red hair and a big smile and blue eyes that laugh as she talks.

Beth trained me for two years. One day during training, she spoke about her career. "I'm nearing thirty-five and it's about time to stop competing, but there's one thing I really want. In all the competitions, I always take second. No matter what I do or how I eat or how hard I train, I get second. I just don't want to retire from competing without coming in first at least once." Beth's final competition was in six weeks.

We talked about what it might take for Beth to win, and she hired me to coach her. I knew my job had nothing to do with training her physically. She was already brilliant at that. She and I had several meetings. We did processes to unlock her appetite and desire and completions to clear out her thinking. I cannot say when it happened, but there came a moment when she was speaking about her life and finally discovered what was holding her back. Though she was a great person, she really believed she was second class. This weighed her down tremendously, so I told her it could not possibly be the truth. She was relieved and began to understand why she had never placed first in competition.

She could see herself standing on stage to be judged, unconsciously thinking she was second class and somehow convincing the judges—though she did her best and never said a word to them—that second was the right place for her. She began to realize that she was getting the exact prize she was inadvertently asking for. All of a sudden the judges were not in charge of her win;

she was. I asked her to imagine that the judges were willing to give her any prize she wanted. She lit up and went to work.

Over the remaining weeks till the competition, I had Beth do the completion process on every time in her life she had come in second—in her family, her school, romances, and so on. Simultaneously, she began to build her appetite by imagining a first-class life. I asked her to spend the hours while she trained each day imagining how a first-class life would be for her—where she would live, how she would dress, who her friends would be, how she would think, who she would be. Most importantly, she was to imagine how she would feel if she knew that no matter where she was or what circumstance she was in, she was first class and no one could take that away from her.

As she fixed that image in her mind, memories of other times when she had chosen less than she wanted popped up. She did completions on them. Compromises she made occurred to her and more completions followed.

Her next assignment was to listen to the way she spoke to herself and to other people and to recognize when she was speaking in a less than first-class manner. The result was a slew of completions on the way she acknowledged herself, how she took compliments, and the conversations she had in her head that kept her right where she was.

I also coached Beth to make a physical declaration of being first class by visualizing the energy that went with being first class radiating from her body in a powerful aura enveloping everyone around her. She practiced going through her days projecting that aura, and I asked her to notice the difference in the way people treated her or responded to her. She visualized the judges giving her what she asked for. This time what she was asking for was first place.

Beth visualized how she would do her program at the competition in a first-class style. She added this visualization to her physical workout program and activated her visualization with every push of a weight. She told me that she had picked very hot music for her final posing routine. She could see the color of the posing outfit she would wear and how it would set off her skin and her red hair. She could see herself onstage and feel herself being the center of attention and turning up the voltage in the audience. Rather than seeing herself responding to the judges (second-class style), she could see them responding to her (first-class style). Finally, she could see herself taking first place and she imagined how it would feel. At one point, she called me and said, "Damn, man, I'm hot!" I started to laugh. I know the truth when I hear it.

Finally, the day of the competition arrived. Beth's close friend and I were there to support her and watch the trials. Beth passed the initial trials with flying colors. At last the finals arrived. There were five contestants in her weight class. Two women posed, and for us the tension mounted. Then Beth was announced to the pounding rhythm of George Thoroughgood's "Bad to the Bone," a driving and sexually charged rock and roll anthem about strutting your stuff, getting what you want, and having the time of your life doing it.

Beth strutted onto the stage in a black posing outfit that showed off her tan, muscled body. The look on her face was dazzling as she hit her required poses. Beth was smiling from ear to ear, eyes flashing everywhere she looked, owning her body, the stage, and the audience. This was the most electrifying performance we had seen. Beth was telling the truth: she was bad to the bone. The audience went berserk. They loved her and cheered throughout her performance. The shouting, clapping, and whistling went on and on even after she left the stage.

You know the ending. Beth took first place in her weight class and qualified for the national competitions for the first time in her life at age thirty-five—well beyond the peak of most bodybuilding careers. At a celebration meal after the competition, Beth and I spoke about her plans. "That's it," she said. "I don't really care about going to the nationals. They are just another round of even more grueling workouts, severe diets, and insane competition. I'm retiring tonight with my first place, but I'm walking away knowing that I'm first class and that's something I'm not retiring from."

Beth's story is powerful because she was able to see what had been invisible—namely, that she was owned by a condition of "second class-ness" that lived in her thoughts, her beliefs, the way she communicated, and the energy she generated—that colored everything, even what she asked for. Without seeing that, she had no power to change the condition. When she opened up an inquiry into the truth that would set her free, she finally had a shot at her most cherished dream.

If you tell the truth, moments like this are what we are really here for. They make life worth living. Telling the truth is the essence of what is feminine because it creates and gives birth to new life, a universal source of celebration.

The Way of Power

The dominator model has had the far-reaching effect of making people believe that power resides in how much force you can exert to get your own way, especially over others. Have you ever noticed that every time you force yourself to do something that is "good for you," even though your heart and spirit are not in it, you set up a condition in which you are at odds with yourself? More often than not, this condition results in not being able to accomplish beautifully what you are forcing yourself to do.

The most powerful leaders are the ones who have the power to open new realities. When you tell the truth, you voice something that has not been said before and create a new reality for yourself, making you an authentic leader in your own life. When you speak your truth to others, you open the possibility of deeper relationships and partnerships. When you give another person the opportunity to tell the truth about something in her life, you give the possibility of freedom to another. Empowerment is one of the great truths about leadership, because it sets everyone, starting with you, free.

First-class people require a voice, a way to speak about what is important to them that matches their elevated status. The next chapter is an exploration of the third key to empowering leadership, voice. In it, you will discover the power to break the silence that women live with. In breaking the seal on your own voice, you dissolve the condition of silence in which women have been trained to live by the dominator model. You discover the power to announce, to call forth, and to create out of nothing except your own godly power, as in "In the beginning was the Word …."

Chapter 8

The Key of Voice

In rural China, it is said that when you knock on the door of a household where all the men are out and only women are at home, you will hear one of the women say, "Go away. No one is home." The sense of being someone individually and personally and having a voice to articulate visions and desires, which are starved in most women, are strikingly lacking in these rural Chinese women.

Unfortunately, the names women traditionally have been taught to call themselves are "no one," "the wife," "Mom," "just a housewife." Women most often change their surname when they marry because it is traditional for a woman to marry into the family of her husband (the more important person). As I mentioned in Chapter 7, when a man enters the room—any man—the automatic reaction of the women is to stop what they are doing and focus on him, regardless of the importance of their meeting or the unimportance of the man. They lose their voice and with it their power because second-class people are trained to respond to and handle whatever a first-class person wants. In other words, first-class people generate; second-class people comply, as in "The King commands; the people obey."

It has been a particularly delicate process to teach and consult with women on leadership in The Feminine Principle, because most women have been trained to defer to me, rather than partner with me. For this reason, in recent years I have had courses on The Feminine Principle for women only, and have encouraged them to add whatever they want to express, including disagreement. Disagreement is particularly difficult when a woman has been trained to have no voice around a man. It is not disagreement itself that is important. It's the right to voice opinions, views, or experiences as an individual in one's own right that makes all the difference.

When malnutrition or starvation is present, the first and only thing to do is to provide nourishment until there is a return to health. Without that return to health, all the potential in the world will lie dormant and remain untapped. When nourishment is provided—something you can do by calling on appetite and desire and by digesting or completing what you have already experienced—the natural reanimation of the human spirit occurs.

The most profound change that occurs is that silence becomes intolerable, and the desire to speak and be heard reawakens. Speaking is one of the mightiest things you can do. When you speak out loud, you create a physical wave of energy that is received by the people to whom you are speaking. More importantly, the sound of your own physical voice calls forth your *voice*, which is a spiritual power. Voice is the expression of your own personal spirit saying what is important and what is required for you to live the life that you know you want. Voice is a function of saying what you are committed to, and by saying, activating it in yourself and others.

Telling the truth is one way to find your voice. This chapter is an exploration of three other ways to find and use your voice to generate the leadership and results you want. They are …

1. Breaking the barrier of "no permission."
2. Making declarations.
3. Discovering the power of command, free of domination or control.

Breaking the Barrier of No Permission

Permission to speak outside the role of wife and mother, permission to disagree with men, permission to think for yourself, permission to say what you really want to say, permission to put yourself first, permission to be magnificent—these basic freedoms, which men enjoy automatically, require systematic development for most women.

Some women I have worked with argue that they have an "emotional block" against giving themselves permission. They want to spend time working on the block to find out how it got there, where they were traumatized, who made them that way, and the like. It is true that in many cases, women have been beaten, threatened, and put down for giving themselves permissions that are normally assigned to men. To be able to express their thoughts and feelings about these experiences is liberating and is a quality of voice. To keep going over the incidents or feelings is a trap.

The one and only permanent cure for the condition of "no permission" is to be able to think and behave freely. To make the internal and behavioral changes that give you more freedom is something only you can do. At the same time, to be trained, coached, and encouraged to try out new behaviors and get feed-back on them from people who are already competent is one of the most powerful things you can do to get where you are going. There is no need to reinvent the wheel when there are others who can show you how to have more of what you want with ease, speed, and elegance. This book is a form of coaching. It is my best attempt to educate and guide you into a new and more fulfilling way to live, even if we will never meet in person. At the very least, a circle of friends who can cheer you on and catch you when you stumble is absolutely essential. It is also the essence of what is feminine.

As you get more competent and have more successes, the internal states that you thought of as your "block" change or disappear. This is what practical education and coaching are all about.

There is a wonderful woman named Anna who did not finish high school and spent the bulk of her life raising her children and taking care of her husband. When her husband was laid off in his fifties, there was not enough income to sustain the family. Not having worked outside her home for thirty years, Anna found the idea of getting a job daunting. But times being what they were, she was willing to go outside her comfort zone and go out into the workplace.

The mother of her son's best friend worked in a local hospital in the personnel department. Anna's son offered to ask his friend's mother, Betty, if there were any openings at the hospital. Anna told her son to ask Betty if there were jobs in the hospital kitchen, because that's all she thought she was qualified for. Betty, knowing how gracious and people-oriented Anna was, recommended instead that Anna apply for a position as a receptionist at the hospital's information desk. Though terrified, Anna applied for the job.

When confronted with the need for a high school education, Anna faltered, but Betty encouraged her to "think creatively" and consider her life experiences as the equivalent of several high school diplomas. Anna checked the high school diploma box "Yes." Betty explained that the most important part of the job was to warmly greet and give information to hospital visitors—something that Anna already knew how to do. Within a month, Anna had learned the job. For nearly seventeen years, she was a devoted employee and the light of the information area. When she retired, many executive, medical, and administrative staff of the hospital attended her retirement party.

When I interviewed her, she said, "The greatest thing that happened to me was that I took Betty's advice and applied for a better job than I thought I could do. When I practiced using the equipment and worked out the routine, everything just clicked into place. Even after all these years, I am still amazed that I gave myself permission to apply for that job. It's one of the best things that ever happened to me."

Discover Where You Have No Permission

You can use your appetite and desire to give yourself a lot more permission than you are used to. As you practice appetite and desire, you might notice that you begin to cover the same territory over and over. When this occurs, you can open more capacity by asking any of these questions:

- What do I have no permission to want?
- What do I have no permission to think?
- What do I have no permission to feel?
- What do I have no permission to say?
- What do I have no permission to have?
- What do I have no permission to do?
- What do I have no permission to be?

Any one of these questions will open whole new worlds of appetite and desire. You can ask them about categories from the State of Nourishment Survey or about anything else that is important to you. When you ask what you have no permission for, you access information that has been closed off to you. It lies in the subconscious, rather than the conscious. The question of what you have no permission for is designed to bypass what you normally think or are aware of and make you inquire into something deeper, more emotional, and less apparent. Often the answers will take you by surprise because they are not logical, but intuitive.

Take the category "leadership." Here are items that are common to women when they ask the questions of "no permission." Add items that are specific to you regarding leadership.

- No permission to want: to take charge, to be seen as a leader, a lot more income, to be proud of myself in public, to be seen as a "bitch," to tell people what to do, to be disliked, to take a public stand, to have too much attention, to be powerful.
- No permission to think: that I'm worth it, that I am better than someone else, that I could be a star, that I am beautiful, that my body is fine the way it is, that I'm smart enough, that I am seen as a leader by others, that I have something

to say, that I could do a better job than the person who is leading, that I have charisma.

- No permission to feel: powerful, sexy, extraordinary, angry, loved and appreciated for who I am, that I'm fine the way I am, immune to criticism, proud of myself, all my emotions and let them out.

- No permission to say: what I need, exactly what I mean, that I am the best, that people should follow me, that I'm being treated unfairly, that I need help, that I was first in line, that I'm powerful, that I have a right to be heard, that I'm fine without a man; no permission to say no, goodbye, or that I'm done.

- No permission to have: more fun in my work, more money, a raise, more power than men around me, respect for my talents, better ideas than other people, a real partner, my light shine brighter than other people's, my life the way I want it until my kids are grown.

- No permission to do: what I really want, things that are just for me, things that other people may not like, activities on my own, adventurous things; no permission to take risks, to do nothing, to daydream, to stop eating when I'm full, to brag, to laugh loud, to tell an off-color joke, to make the first move.

- No permission to be: honest about what I want and don't want, really proud of myself, sensuous, the person who dis-agrees, a sovereign woman, in charge of my company, lead-ing the way with my husband; no permission to be angry, sad, unhappy, frank, or fragile.

It is vitally important to be honest with yourself. It is not im-portant to try to discover where the lack of permission started or whose fault it was. That will get you nowhere.

Break the Seal of Bondage

Every time you discover something else for which you have no permission, you break the seal of your own unconscious bondage. Then you can do completions that digest the past and give you an opportunity for something new or expanded.

For example, if you discover you have no permission to say exactly what you mean, you can do a completion on your current level of saying what you mean or on your freedom to say what you mean. Locate yourself in a place of having (current level, freedom to) rather than in a place of loss (the problem of). To locate yourself in a place of having creates a focus on more of what you want, not what you don't want.

The Feminine Principle is about opening to more. When you open to (focus on) more of what you don't have, you give more energy and importance to what is lacking. When you open to more of what you do have, even in very small quantities, you give more energy and importance to that. What you invest in gives you a return.

When you break the seal of silence, you may feel emotional surges. When you discover what you have no permission for, especially anger or fear or sadness, they naturally find expression. This is simply an emptying of what has been stored up in you with no freedom to express it. Emptying releases the pressure you live with and brings you to a deeper state of freedom and balance. It is important to give yourself the freedom to express whatever emotion opens. At the same time, it is not necessary to dramatize or wallow in it.

Sorry No More

After completing the list of no-permission, you may feel that you have done something wrong by wanting something other than what you have. Women apologize endlessly. It is part of the culture of being second class. (Men, on the other hand, almost never apologize, even when they desperately need to.)

This morning I received an e-mail about a conference call I had scheduled with a woman with twenty years' executive experience in business. Though I had clearly made a mistake regarding the day of the call, she apologized and said that she had written today in her appointment calendar, but she must have gotten it wrong. I had to argue with her to convince her that I, not she, had made the mistake.

You could have a breakthrough in leadership simply by observing how many times in a day you say you are sorry and giving yourself a day off from it. It would be an instructive experience to go through a day and not feel sorry for anything and not say you are sorry to anyone. To go through life being sorry is a quality of being second class.

Apology, on the other hand, is a necessary and useful thing. It repairs what may have been damaged. This is different from being sorry. Women are taught to be sorry, as in worthless, inferior, poor; men are taught to find out who is to blame and punish them, as in someone's wrong and they will pay for it. Apology is acknowledging that a mistake has been made, expressing regret for any damage that has been caused, and taking action to rectify it. Apology without action to rectify the mistake is no apology at all.

Apology is a state of responsibility that has nothing to do with blame or punishment. In a state of responsibility, you have the ability to respond to what is happening in a powerful, effective way. It is the antithesis of being "less than," or groveling. It is active, powerful, and healing. It is the ultimate in first-class behavior because it takes being big and being open to accept responsibility.

Some years ago, in a remarkable turnabout from the way business and politics operate in the United States, the president of Japan Airlines—a man—publicly apologized for the crash of one of JAL's flights and expressed his deep regret for the suffering this disaster had caused. He understood in his core what real leadership is—personally taking responsibility for everything that happens on your watch, whether you had anything directly to do with it or not. After his apology he resigned his position and made way for a new person to be in charge. He obviously was not to blame for the crash, but he responded with what was necessary to set things right. Compare this to the endless evasions that leaders in this country make when confronted with a mistake; the difference is like night and day.

At the end of the millennium, the Pope made headlines around the world when he publicly apologized for the Crusades, the Inquisition, the mistreatment of Jews, and a host of other offenses his church had committed over the last thousand years. He asked for forgiveness on behalf of his church—a perfect example of full responsibility seldom seen in men.

In the United States, our business and political leaders apologize only when they are forced to because they are caught red-handed or with their pants down—sometimes literally. More often than not, they tough it out and express regret only at being caught or deny their mistake to the end. This dominator model of leadership is ruthlessly trained into boys and is the antithesis of responsibility. It is a bully's way of going through life.

You do absolutely nothing wrong by wanting what you want. In fact, you open your capacity for wanting a larger life and make that available for anyone connected to you—namely everyone. The Feminine Principle, being inclusive and focused on nourishment, is naturally generous and expansive.

A final few words on the subject of permission. You would be safe in assuming that your areas of lack of permission are not unique or even unusual; it's good to remember the principle that life is holographic and connected. For example, when I speak to associations of women, I know that I may not really have their permission to speak to them because I'm a man. Their initial reaction is "What could a man possibly know about The Feminine Principle?" I also know that they may not have permission, because of their training, to ask me about this directly, so I normally start my speech by asking the question myself. It's always good for a laugh, breaks the ice, and enables me to answer directly what they have no permission to ask. There is a very feminine principle at work here: whatever you include, you have the power to use. Whatever you exclude uses you.

Making Declarations

"We hold these truths to be self-evident …" So begins one of the most powerful documents ever written, a document that launched a nation that has grown into the most powerful in history. The Declaration of Independence was basically written by a group of businesspeople, leaders in their community who took a stand for the end of oppression and something brand new. This document and the Constitution have become models for people all over the world who desire freedom. They are at the heart of our greatness as a country and as a people, because they create the American model or mindset, a system of beliefs that have proven to be extremely powerful. (Models create reality.)

You, too, can make declarations that have the power to change your life and alter your reality. You have the power to make declarations that make you great. You do not need any special education or particular religious training or political affiliation. You simply need your voice, which, thank goodness, comes as standard equipment on human beings. It is important to remember that when I say "voice" I mean the quality of spirit that allows you to make clear who you are, what you desire, and what you are committed to. Primarily, people use their physical voice to express their spiritual *voice*, but you can express your voice through writing, as in the Declaration of Independence; through pictures, as in "one picture is worth a thousand words"; and through gestures and body language, as in "when she smiled and opened her arms to embrace me, I knew I was forgiven." All these ways to communicate allow your *voice* to be "heard."

Speak Your Word

The fundamental action of declaration is to speak your word as a stand you take, to live in and deliver on whatever reality you are creating. For example, "I'm having my own business this year" or "That's the last time I'll ever settle for less" or "The only thing I'll respond to is the truth that sets me free." When you use the power of declaration to take a stand, you locate yourself in a place of power and can begin to construct a world that is the fulfillment of that stand. (More on this in the next chapter.)

Declaration does not owe its power to prior evidence or guarantees. It is, rather, a creation from nothing but your word. Declaration at the deepest spiritual level is the very thing that Jewish and Christian Scriptures say God used to create the entire universe. "And God said, 'Let there be light …'" This is not just a saying. It is an expression of the fundamental process of calling anything new into existence. Word is what creates. If you have no power to speak your word, you have no power.

When you stood in front of friends and family and declared with your beloved that you would henceforth be married, the world around you changed in a flash, based on giving your word and taking a stand about it. The officiating person at your wedding was only an official witness, not someone who married you. What you say is powerful and creative.

Like the electricity that runs through your home, word is a power that is neither intrinsically good nor bad. Like electricity, it can light you up or electrocute you. You decide. You have the power in your word to take a stand for your glory or your suffering. You elevate or condemn yourself by what you say to yourself and others about you. Your silence is also your word, which, in most cases, is taken as your assent to go along with whatever is on the table.

When the national silence about our participation in Vietnam was shattered by tens of thousands of priests, rabbis, ministers, and grandmothers marching in the streets and declaring that they had had enough, things changed. When enough women demanded the right to vote and marched in the streets for it, things changed. When African Americans walked the streets by the thousands and refused to be silenced by threats of violence, things changed. When women burnt their bras en masse and declared their freedom from the domination of men (in reality, the dominator cultural model), the very times themselves changed and are still changing.

Sometimes, when I listen to the way word is used by our leaders to confront, intimidate, and threaten, I cringe. Though the language of and emphasis on violence and darkness are given much airtime, it is time for word to be used for its original purpose, which is to create the world that human beings universally want.

Six Ways to Unleash the Power of Declaration

Declaration opens the game and provides a compass for getting where you are going. If you declare that you will open your own law office by the end of this year, you act in a completely different way than you would if you said you were staying put. Your priorities shift based on your declarations. Your internal conversations change and the conversations you have with other people change to match. Even the people change. Some, who have no interest in your declaration, disappear. Others appear, often as if by magic, galvanized and inspired by the power of your word.

There are six stages in using and releasing the power of declaration, starting with telling the truth and ending in action. Use them as a guide and adapt them to work for you.

1. **Get clear about who you are and what you are up to.**

   Tell the truth to get to the heart of the matter. This may be the single most important thing you can do to put your life on course. When I told the truth and realized that I was not here to make a living but to invent a new future for the world my children will inherit, something fundamental shifted in me. I opened to opportunities that could never have existed for me otherwise. Maybe they existed in the world at large, but I could not have taken advantage of them. I would have no reason to. What you declare gives you the "reason to." It also gives you access to the world that you declare and the opportunities that live in that world. This is a profound power.

2. Make your declaration.

Say it out loud to yourself in the mirror often. Practice saying your word until you can speak about it without hesitation. (If you experience hesitation, ask yourself where you have no permission and do completions on whatever comes up.) Write your declaration down and put it up where you can look at it all through the day.

Declaration is you in your glory, saying the way it will be for you and holding yourself accountable for it. Declaration makes you a leader in your own private universe, bringing your world into existence. *Declare* comes from the Latin verb *declarare*, which means "to make clear." When you declare, you make your intention clear to yourself and others.

3. Tell other people your declaration.

Make it a practice to include your declaration in your conversations. At the beginning, this may seem strange or uncomfortable; being so forthright often is. You will become aware, however, that as people hear and respond to your word, its power increases and gains momentum—no matter what they say about it.

Declaration is the first act of leadership. It is what elicits participation and action. Without something to align with, there is no coherence, whether in ideas or people. Declaration magnetizes the people, opportunities, and experiences that are in harmony with what you have declared. When you declare to yourself, you are leading in your own life. When you declare to others, you are leading publicly.

You make declarations all the time. "I'll be in the office by 9:15." "Yes, we'll be at your party and would love to bring dessert." "We'll do what it takes to save a down payment for a house by the end of the year." The point is to make them consciously and to pay attention to what you are promising with your declaration. Your declaration is your word, and to live by it is at the heart of integrity. In California, people normally show up ten to fifteen minutes late no matter what. Frankly, it is better to declare that you will be late or to declare the time you will actually arrive than it is to make a false declaration. Through my experience working with thousands of people, I've come to believe that there is a "witness" in each of us that listens to every word we say, whether we think so or not, whether we say it out loud or not.

4. **Make declarations that involve some risk.**

    Put yourself somewhat outside your current ability to produce and in the position of needing to stretch to accomplish what you say. This is a dance that you have to learn to do with yourself but you can certainly get feedback from people you trust. If you declare only for what is within reach, you simply are saying that you will take what is already there.

    A leading declaration is one that leaves a gap between who you are and what you can accomplish now and who you could be and what you could accomplish if you opened yourself to new powers and new pathways. Declarations that are somewhat out of your comfort zone compel you to think differently, ask for more help than you are used to, and even take some risks.

    One thing is certain about effective leadership: great leaders make declarations that put them at risk, and they find within themselves the wherewithal to produce the results. You could say that to be a leader is to live in the land of risk because there is no certainty when you declare for something new. Finding the wherewithal within yourself is the name of the game. It is also an extraordinary way to grow and express your greatness.

5. **Take action on your declarations.**

    Declarations are magic, but they are not genie-in-the-lamp magic. The real magic of declarations is that they call you into action beyond your current capacity or comfort zone. Actions are what put you on the playing field. Action generates magnetism and attracts support. Sometimes you win and sometimes you lose, but the fun is to be on the field and in action. Discover for yourself that you would rather spend one hour on the playing field—whatever it is for you—than sit in the stands day after day and watch others star in their lives.

6. **Stay on the field and don't give up.**

   In the many years I have coached extraordinary women, I have found that just at the moment when they could win, there is an almost diabolical urge to quit. Often a major breakthrough or epiphany is preceded by an impulse to bolt or give up. But if you stay on the "playing field," you will pass through the impulse to bolt (or go back to what you know) and you will get where you are going. Tenacity makes the world sit up and take notice. The ultimate declaration is "I will not budge until my word is fulfilled." That is what makes leadership difficult. It is also what makes leadership deeply rewarding and people who play the leadership game profoundly alive.

What You Own, You Can Command

The word *command* comes from the Latin *commandare*, which means "to entrust," quite literally "to put trust in." Want a commanding presence? Want the power to command? Want to be someone in whom others put their trust? In The Feminine Principle, there is only one way to do that authentically—namely, to take a leadership position in your own life by telling the truth and acting on it, and by demonstrating what you want or expect from other people. This will give you a command presence that everyone can trust. It will also give you power that is unassailable because it lives in you as your own personal demonstration of a declaration that you have made. Nobody can take that away from you. The most powerful way to lead is by owning who and what you are and using this ownership to empower yourself and other people. Most people willingly own their inferiority. They use it as a way to take themselves off the hook for the visions and projects that would actually move life forward. To own your magnificence is a completely different thing. It is a statement of capacity. *Magnificence* comes from the Latin word *magnus*, meaning "great" or "large." Know people who are "larger than life"? It's all a matter of capacity, which you have the power to grow.

Want to get people rolling for what you believe? Move and inspire them and people will produce results that are nothing short of miraculous. What moves and inspires is personal demonstration. Demonstration is important because it is you owning your life, your actions, and your results, and living in acknowledgment of what you have declared.

The power of ownership is shown clearly by the role of emotion in leadership. The dominator version of The Masculine Principle has no ownership of emotion, one of the central experiences that enable you to recognize the truth. It denies emotion, and with that denial, loses its power to command or empower an essential aspect of what makes human beings act with greatness and valor. No wonder people who operate from the ruthlessness of the dominator model feel cold and less than truthful. They are.

The Feminine Principle is not about being emotional, but neither is it stopped by emotion. It is simply inclusive of it; it owns emotion. Because of this, feminine leadership moves and inspires, rather than coerces or frightens. For feminine leaders, the style of leading is one of the key factors that underpin their ability to produce the results they want. If you have emotion—and *all* human beings do—The Feminine Principle encourages you to own it, use it to recognize the truth, and express it to empower yourself and others.

The single greatest characteristic for which women in leadership positions are faulted is that they are too emotional. Women in the dominator model are left with the choice of turning off their emotional response—a source of power—or being thrown out of the game. The point of leadership in the feminine style is to have your emotions and use them to empower everyone around you.

Lynne Twist is a talented and brilliant leader who was born into wealth and privilege. She could have spent her life any way she wanted. The way she has chosen to spend it is by raising tens of millions of dollars for projects that move humanity forward into a more equitable, sustainable world. Having been to dozens of meetings that she has led over the years, I can personally attest to the power of her leadership in fundraising. I have made many pledges and written many checks in response to her leadership.

Lynne told me several years ago that for years she tried to suppress her tears when she led meetings. She was embarrassed by her emotion and thought it was not appropriate. Then she discovered something that changed everything. A co-worker said that when Lynne cried, it was clear that the meeting was working beautifully because Lynne cried when she was moved and inspired by the material of the meeting. When she knew she could relax and include emotion in her meetings—in fact, use her tears as a barometer for the caliber of the meeting—she was set free. Rather than hamper her, her tears provided the power to move and inspire others. To include emotion and use it to nourish your creations is feminine and powerful.

Own or Be Owned

Certain communications are difficult because they are highly charged with emotion, have the potential to do damage, or are foreign to the way we have been taught that it is acceptable to interact with one another. To be in leadership, from time to time you have to have conversations, make requests, and ask or answer questions that you would prefer not to.

You can turn these situations into wins for all concerned by creating a style of communicating that includes up front any condition that might be a problem. Though sometimes embarrassing, these conditions are best handled by being straightforward and addressing the potential hazards you know are there.

You can set up how the other person listens to you by saying, for
example ...

> "This is very difficult to say, but it is important for me to tell
> you."

> "I often cry when I tell this story because it is so moving.
> Nothing is wrong."

> "When I am this angry, I often walk away, but you are impor-
> tant to me, so I want to stay and talk about this."

> "Every voice in my head is telling me not to say this because
> you will think I'm silly (petty, stupid, etc.)."

> "I need to have a conversation with you and I am afraid of
> your reaction."

When you acknowledge up front whatever "cards" you are
holding, you demonstrate generosity with the other person. You
set up how the other person listens to you by opening yourself and
being vulnerable, rather than protecting yourself. Others begin to
understand that it takes real courage for you to open to say what
you have to say. By your actions, you invite them to be generous
in the way they listen to you. Most people respect generosity, no
matter how difficult the material, because they have also been
in situations where it has been difficult to say things. More connection and more relatedness are established. Things go more
smoothly because generosity always creates better results.

The important thing is to say what you have to say in relationship and in connection. Have the intention to empower the other
person as well as to get what you have to say off your chest. That
is where the rubber of leadership meets the road.

Empowerment Leadership: The End Goal

The fourth kind of leadership, empowerment, integrates the ability to command, the ability to pioneer new territory by inquiring
into what is already known and creating innovations, the ability to

demonstrate leadership in your own life, and the ability to give that leadership away to others. This kind of leadership has the power and the intention to create more leaders who can demonstrate leadership in their own lives and share a new future. It is conscious, deliberate leadership at the highest level.

One such leader is Dr. Patricia Taylor. Her book, *Expanded Orgasm*, and her lecture and workshop series have opened new frontiers in lovemaking and consciousness for thousands and thousands of people. Patti spent many years on Wall Street as a commodity trader. Then, out of the blue she began to have experiences of intense energy in her body that took her to different states of consciousness. Patti thought she was going crazy. It took her many years to understand and use this energy, which people in Eastern spiritual traditions call *kundalini*. As she opened to the experience of what was happening to her, she found a pathway into a completely new world.

Years later, an acknowledged and respected trailblazer in her field, Patti has become an authority on the access to consciousness that touching and pleasure provide. It is her command of the subject in her own body and soul that give Patti the power to broach this very delicate subject with assurance and grace and open it as a public conversation. To declare her stand for pleasure and consciousness and to empower men and women to have more consciousness through their communion are groundbreaking achievements.

"When people first come to me they think I'm all about sex," Patti said when I interviewed her. "They don't realize that I'm interested in sex in so far as it provides a window into the world of spirit and greater consciousness. Right now I am inventing a brand-new language for lovemaking that is free from the baggage about sex we carry from the past. Lovemaking for me is not a euphemism for sex. It is a creative process. I don't know exactly where it's going. It's the exploration and the journey that are compelling to me."

Patti speaks for millions and millions of people who are awakening to their own personal leadership, whatever the subject or area of
concern. In the journey of leadership, free from the dominator effect that has suppressed and silenced every single one of us in ways
seen and unseen, the path opens as you go. To take the next step by
completing something from your past, by increasing your appetite
and celebrating your desire, by granting yourself permission where
there was none, and by finding your voice and declaring for your
future, you add to the swelling wave of what development experts,
global strategists, and political leaders are calling "the new human
agenda." This agenda includes targets for progress in health, education, the empowerment of women, preservation of the environment,
and stabilization of population growth. To command leadership
in this new agenda for humanity, from your own personal authority, gives practical meaning to Mahatma Gandhi's "Be the world
you want." One by one as people become the world they want, that
larger world takes shape and comes into existence.

We have the power to express our commitments by taking a
stand for them. Taking a stand is like laying a foundation. It gives
you a place from which to think, to act, and to measure your results against. Stance has real magic in it. As the poet Goethe said,
"... the moment one definitely commits oneself, then providence
moves too. All sorts of things occur to help one that would never
otherwise have occurred. A whole stream of events issues from the
decision, raising in one's favor all manner of unforeseen incidents,
meetings and material assistance ...."

The next chapter investigates the magic of stance and the power
of *reinvention*—the conscious redesign of your personal strategy to
match your voice and empower your stand. When you expand your
capacity, tell the truth, and open your voice, you are not the old you
plus some new things, anymore than a woman is a little girl plus
puberty. A new human being comes into existence whose visions,
perceptions, and actions are correlated to something entirely different from the place you were before. It is in this power to create

yourself anew, to redefine yourself in relation to the future you are committed to, that the future you want stops being a wish and starts being a reality. The next chapter will show you how to activate this profound power.

Chapter 9

The Key of Stance

To quickly review Chapter 2, models are systems of belief meant to explain, predict, and/or control phenomena. They create reality by consensus when enough people hold a system of belief in common. They are human inventions. Models are not true (I'm using *true* in the traditional sense, which is completely different from *true* meaning *having the power to set you free*)—that is, they do not exist in an absolute sense, but they do have the power to create a perceptual background against which phenomena become real. For example, in Western Europe, diseases were thought to be caused by "humours," four liquids in the body that, left unbalanced, caused disease. Even God's wrath was thought to be a chief cause of disease, a belief held to be true by some people even today. With the invention of the microscope and the discovery of microbes, a new model was born that has saved millions of lives that would have been lost within the old model. From where we are today, we have no idea what will happen when enough people use the New Feminine Principle and come into their wholeness.

The final key, stance, is what enables you to place yourself firmly in the center of your truth and declare it with your voice. It is the "posture" you assume toward yourself and the world, making who you are and the model you live clear to everyone around you. Stance is the inner place of courage and commitment within which you plant your feet and take your outer stand for what is important to you. It is the final springboard into a life of leadership.

To use the key of stance, it is necessary to understand that your very idea of who you are resides in a model that can be changed

at will, though often not without deep commitment and persever-
ance. You must also know that there are models within models.
The model of The Feminine Principle as it is now gives you the
background against which you know who you are as a woman;
however, the final "creation" of who you are lies in you yourself, in
your personal stance, regardless of the model's power to steer you
in a certain direction. Otherwise, there would never be anyone who
"marched to the beat of a different drummer."

This chapter shows you how to reinvent your personal stance
and start from a brand-new place in your life. When you start from
a new place, your whole perception of who you are and what is
available to you changes. You gain the power to invent yourself, to
write a new story about your life, and to create a new future into
which you can live. Nothing could be more female than to "invent"
new life in your body. Nothing could be more feminine than to invent a new spirit of life in yourself. It is my hope that when you reinvent yourself you will take a stand for a New Feminine Principle
that has the capacity, truth, and voice to invoke a new future for
yourself and the world around you.

The Invention of Personal Strategy

Strategy is the science or art of military command as applied to
the overall planning and conduct of large-scale combat opera-
tions. Strategic thinking is a powerful way of planning, unfortunately imbedded in a model that was originally invented for the
most severe kind of competition, war—the very antithesis of The
Feminine Principle. It is important to reclaim strategy for The New
Feminine Principle and use it in a way that promotes leadership in
the feminine style.

If you want to use strategy, you must reinvent it by taking it off
the battlefield and putting it into the kind of leadership that does
not compete or attack. Fortunately, if you look into the root of
strategy, you discover that it comes from the Greek *strategia*, the

office of a general. *Office* is *a position of authority or trust*, and *authority* comes from a root word that means "to increase, to create."

In The New Feminine Principle, you can hold the office of leader by (1) trusting yourself to use your voice to take a stand for your leadership, and (2) creating your leadership as something that opens you and increases your power to be effective and to empower others. Every time you take a stand, you create an avenue into a new future, with a whole new set of realities and *truths* that may or may not have anything to do with what has gone before. You leave the domain of logical projection and you enter the domain of creation.

Taking a Personal Stand

You can take a stand for anything that moves and inspires you about your own life or the world at large: for example, inner peace, peace in your home life, and peace globally. You can (and do) stand for many things simultaneously: for example, a nourishing spiritual practice, your health, the health of your family, equal rights, ecological balance, political freedom, beauty, close friendships. The list of what you can stand for is endless.

Here are six ways to take and declare a stand for leadership:

1. I am a leader in … (for example, my community, family, church, neighborhood, business, or organization).
2. I am a leader of … (for example, people, women, young or old people, citizens in my town, my business, my social or professional group, or my family).
3. I am leading in/demonstrating … (for example, personal or financial freedom, forward thinking, equality for all, power, happiness, voice, passion, creativity).
4. I am empowering others in … (for example, self-expression, intellectual development, voice, competence, or career).

5. I am standing for ... (for example, leadership in the feminine style, the truth, inclusion, deeper relationship, my family's thriving, a breakthrough in sales).

6. I am pioneering ... (for example, a New Feminine Principle, new traditions in our family, new opportunities for women).

When you live your life from your stance, you stop being owned by your past, your personality, your problems, or your circumstances and become your word, as in "In the beginning was the Word ...." This is godly power. Giving your word as a stand is an act of pure creation because it is not dependent on what the circumstances dictate at any particular time. It relies on nothing but what you say and hold yourself to.

The most powerful stands are not in opposition to anything else. There is no battle to do. You are simply powerfully stating where you will locate yourself in regard to any matter. It is like saying, "Here's where I live. If you want to find me, you can find me here. If you want to know where I'm starting from, you can look here."

When you take your stand, you plant yourself firmly and can look out from there. When people know your stand, they know to whom they are talking and they hear everything you say as a commentary on that stand. For example, if you take a stand for co-operation, everything you say or do should forward the action of cooperation. People who know you stand for cooperation can trust you to be speaking from that point of view.

The purpose of your stand is to give you a place to start that enables you to have more of what you are standing for—consistent with the feminine values of nourishment and growth. When you stand for something, you are locating yourself in having it already. The purpose of starting there is to have more experience of whatever you are standing for. For example, when you start from well-being, it is not a thing to get; it is already where you live, even if you have just moved in. What you do or get become expressions of expanding your well-being, not its cause. Your voice and the power to invent a powerful stand are what create your well-being, sometimes even in the face of medical, psychological, or financial evidence to the contrary.

This ability to invent outside of evidence may be the central access to miracles, those sudden, unexplainable occurrences that are the magic of life. It may also explain why many people who have terminal illnesses exemplify extraordinary well-being. Their stand is not about what their body is doing, but rather who they are vis-à-vis their life at that moment.

Leadership as a Personal Stand

Given the relatively small number of people who consciously take stands and act consistently on them, to have a conscious stand and to act from it makes you a leader de facto. Why take a stand for being a leader in The New Feminine Principle? Because The Feminine Principle asserts and values the central ingredients of a great life, not only for you, but for the world around you. When you add the keys of capacity, truth, voice, and stance, you unlock a life of sanity and harmony.

Here is a useful way to think about leadership. In modern times we have made angels anthropomorphic; that is, we have turned them into (for the most part) pretty, blonde, androgynous humans with wings. For Jews, from whom our current Western conception of angels originally sprang, angels are personifications of God's attributes and powers, not separate "people." It is closer to the original meaning and intention to say the "spirit of wisdom" or "the spirit of courage," than to say "the angel of wisdom" or "the angel of courage." The spirit of courage, for example, is the consciousness of courage, the energy of courage, or the state of courage as it manifests in us.

The spirit of leadership is the consciousness, energy, and state of leadership as it lives in you when you invoke and embody it. Leadership grows and shapes you to the degree that you invoke and embody it. What this means in real, practical terms is that when you take a stand and open to leadership, you are not the same person. You are not the old you plus leadership. You are inventing yourself as someone new. At first reading, this may seem foreign. It is certainly not the way we are taught to speak about our lives. At the same time, it is exactly what you do when you get married. You stand up in front of witnesses and take a stand for an entirely new state of relationship with another person. Another way to say it is that you locate yourself in an entirely new place, begin to see things from a new point of view, and take actions that are entirely different from being single. You also start to use different words to describe who you are, such as "Mr. and Mrs.," "husband and wife," and "we." In other words, you become someone new because you consciously invent a new stand that changes major realities from which you were operating. Frankly, if you remain the same old person operating in the same old way, you don't stand a chance of having a successful marriage. Opening to leadership is just like that—a qualitative shift, not just doing things differently. It is a change in the way you "are," not just what you do.

Although people who practice leadership in the dominator model seem like an endless procession of clones, there is no recipe for leadership in The New Feminine Principle because each leader has to give birth to it. As you know if you have children, each child, though made by the same parents, is a completely unique individual. Each leader creates her own unique expression.

In the spiritual life, the world-renowned Mother Teresa declared that in every single person she encountered, she would see Jesus Christ. She took literally Jesus' remarkable stand that "… whatever you do to the least of my brethren, you do to me." The power of her stand never flagged for a moment with lepers, the dying, or heads of state. To hold and live in that stand made her a heroine to millions of people of all faiths and attracted large numbers of women and men who wanted to live in the same stand. Like other great people, this small woman with a large voice took a stand and acted on it until the world began to see it her way.

When you take a stand, your stand provides others with the opportunity to make their own stands and to participate in your stand as colleagues, friends, or partners. Affiliation and connection are natural in The Feminine Principle. When affiliation and connection occur within a powerful stand, their power is magnified. Authentic leaders not only make declarations but also give the people around them the opportunity to be leaders in their own right by making stands that put everyone involved in alignment. This is leadership by empowerment.

Integrity

There is enormous power in being clear where you stand and having others know it. There is even more power knowing that when you take a stand, that stand orients you in a particular direction and your own personal consistency with your stand takes you in the direction *you* said you wanted to go.

In my many years of working with people to express their magnificence, I have discovered that people sometimes use their stands to victimize themselves. They act as if their stand is just one more obligation that they have to bear up under, rather than something they chose. Some people will even pretend that someone else made them take a stand. Nothing could be further from the truth. The only person who can take a stand is you. Nobody can force you, as we have seen time after time with people who would rather die than stand for something they don't believe.

At the heart of this tremendous power to die rather than sell out, to keep going in the face of adversity, and to triumph over seemingly insurmountable obstacles is integrity, *the principle of soundness*. When something is sound, it is complete in its parts, stable in its operation, and sustainable in its nature. Your stance must be sound. It must be an integration of your own values, standards, and beliefs about what is important; otherwise, you actually work against yourself.

There is no greater indicator of integrity than keeping your word. Clearly, from time to time human beings make mistakes. This is not the perfection game; however, if you take a stand and give your word and arbitrarily ignore it whenever you please, you lose the power of your word. People who do this gain the reputation for being weak-willed, hypocritical, even dishonest. On top of that, they lose their moral "compass" and live with the experience of being rudderless.

The most important factor in our distrust and disgust of politicians is that they take a stand to get elected and then do not act with integrity on the stand that put them in office. They may call it "political expediency," but most people call it lack of integrity, pure hypocrisy, or even blatant dishonesty.

The best advice is to take a stand the way you take an oath. Promise to tell the truth. A stand should set you free and give you the power to be the person you want to be. It should be generated from the turn-on of your appetite and desire, but it should also have "knowledge aforethought"—it should be known that you are entering into a sacred contract with yourself that you have every intention of keeping. When a legal contract is violated, the person who violated the contract is normally compelled to pay damages or make restitution in order to restore the integrity of the contract. If you want to avoid paying "damages" like a diminished sense of self-worth, anxiety, worry, and loss of personal power, keep your word to yourself. In the final analysis, it's all you've got to stand on.

Access to Being

There is no path to leadership, because leadership is not someplace to get *to*; it is the place, a stand, you start *from*. The name of the place in consciousness that you start from is called "being." The Japanese call it *sonen*—your innermost thought, attitude, or vibrational level—the totality of you at that moment. There is also no particular thing you have to do to be a leader, because leadership is a state of being, as in *human being*, not *human doing*.

To *be* a leader is an active choice. You cannot make it accidentally. You make it moment by moment, situation by situation. You make the choice to stop what you are doing long enough to ask the question about who you are being and then to act on it.

Leadership is an inquiry you make over and over based on a stand that you made using the power of your voice and speaking your word. Here is the strategic leadership question: "Being a leader, what is the appropriate action to take at this moment?" You have to stop long enough to listen to the answer, not different from asking your computer for information and waiting for it to process your request and give you what you are looking for. It is important to act on the answer you get. Acting on the answer validates your confidence in your own leadership.

Leadership is not about being perfect or getting it right every time—unless *you* say it has to be that way. Leaders make mistakes and use them to empower their leadership by learning from them.

You can use the question "Who am I being at this moment?" to return you to leadership. For example, you are in a particularly difficult situation with your business partner. All you want to do is argue or defend yourself. You have taken a stand to be a leader in The New Feminine Principle, but when you ask "Who am I being at this moment?" you discover that you are being someone who is not leading in connection or partnership. In fact, you are shocked to discover that you are leading in tyranny or pettiness or drama.

You ask yourself what a leader in The New Feminine Principle would do. The answer could be any of a large number of things that would be effective. You could table the issue and come back to it the next day when you are both fresh. You could reaffirm your connection and partnership and acknowledge your partner's efforts. You could open to what your partner has to say and hear it all the way through before commenting. You could agree to disagree and recommend getting an objective opinion. You could look for something brand-new that would satisfy both of you. (Of this last option, real invention is made!)

The point is that when you take a stand, you have the opportunity to reaffirm it every moment in every situation. You have the opportunity to invent new ways to express it. You also give yourself one of life's most enduring gifts—namely, a rich inner dialogue and a relationship with yourself that is filled with creativity and purpose.

Who you are being moves the action forward or limits it. I was visiting with a close friend, Lauri, whose daughter is a singer-songwriter. Her music is unique. It has elements of rock, opera, epic poetry, and hip-hop. One thing is clear—this young woman is not trying to be anyone but herself.

Several record companies have been interested in signing my friend's daughter, Morgan, to their label. Lauri told me that all along she had advised her daughter to listen to the record executives and change her music to be more commercial, if they wanted her to. She said, "I wanted to help get Morgan's foot in the door, but I gave her the wrong advice, by telling her to change who she is to suit the record companies. I was embarrassed to listen to my daughter tell the record executives that she knows she can build a career as an independent artist and songwriter. Morgan told them that if they want to compromise her artistic integrity, she has no intention of talking to them about a record deal." My friend was astonished.

"I apologized to my daughter," Lauri confided, "and told her that I had been advising her to be a person who is willing to compromise her integrity rather than stay true to her artistic vision. I was wrong. I also told my daughter that I have something to learn from her."

As I listened to my friend's story, I was impressed that her daughter is being a leader who stands for artistic integrity. I was also impressed that Lauri is being a mother who demonstrates real leadership by being open enough to admit her mistake to her daughter and learn from her. Contrast this with the last time you heard one of our political leaders come forward with no pressure and admit he or she made a mistake and had something to learn.

Being and Doing

When you distinguish *being* from *doing*, you gain access to a whole new realm of power and effectiveness. Many people whom I have taught or interviewed can be described as "doing machines." It is as if someone put a key in their backs, wound them up, and told them to keep going till they fall over. Even when the river current is taking them where they want to go, they paddle as hard as they can to get there sooner. The world we live in sees them as go-getters. It awards them its highest honor, namely "hard workers"—like medal winners in the puritan Olympics. They feel guilty taking time off, cannot sit still or unwind, and have an endless stream of chatter going on in their heads. They have not mastered the art of pacing themselves, so they stop only when they are exhausted or sick—and sometimes not even then.

When I ask people like this who they are being while they do all the things they do, first they tell me *why* they are doing what they are doing. In other words, they explain their behavior by justifying it. They do not say who they are being because people who are doing machines think that who they are is whatever they are doing. If I ask the question again and again, finally they stop and have nothing to say. Being is invisible to them, because they have forgotten the stand they took for their life, against which what they are doing could be seen clearly as useful or not useful.

When you feel out of control about doing more things, make the choice to stop and ask yourself who you are being at that moment. When you know who you are being, you have the power to change things for the better by going back to your stand and seeing if what you are doing is forwarding it. Completions are a big help. You can do completions on your pace, your freedom to relax, beliefs about what you should be doing, and the like.

Buckminster Fuller—inventor, philosopher, and an authentic American genius—said quite delightfully and accurately that human beings are verbs, not nouns; that is, we are humans in the process of being. When you take a stand by using your voice to declare, "I AM ...," you enter a state of being. You have the power to create heaven or hell by what you declare, as in: "I am (being) first class." "I am (being) not worthy." "I am (being) powerful." "I am (being) stupid." "I am (being) a leader." "I am (being) over-whelmed." "I am (being) loved."

Being and Roles

We live in a world where there is major confusion between who you are and the roles you play. Actors and performers of all kinds are constantly approached by fans who relate to them as the char-acters they play. For many actors, this is a major problem. Rita Hayworth, a movie star of the 1940s, said it brilliantly. "Men want to sleep with Gilda (her most famous screen role) and are disap-pointed when they wake up with me."

We are taught to put every person we meet into a role, a pigeon-hole, especially based on job or career. You ask, "What do you do?" They say their occupation (one role they play) and you immediately pigeonhole them. Accountants are conservative and boring, people who sell used cars are dishonest, clergy are do-gooders, firefighters are heroes, techno-wizards are nerds, etc. This is a good example of the way the dominator model operates to kill off the experience of the connection you could have with the other person, free from their place in the social hierarchy.

You are not the roles you play. You are not your gender. You are not "mom" or "dad." You are not your color, your ethnicity, your socioeconomic status, or any one of a thousand other roles you play. The roles you play are not you any more than the clothes you wear or the house you live in are you. You have roles you play and clothes you wear and houses you live in, but they are not you. You are the actor playing the roles you play. Who you are being as you inhabit each role is who you really are.

Who you are being in each and every role is who *you* say you are, not who others say you are. *Who you say you are* is another way to

say *the stand you have taken.* That is the secret core of leadership in any role or situation.

Here is a true story that moves me to tears whenever I think about it. When my mother died, I had the privilege of delivering her eulogy. Everyone knew Alice in the role of mother—she was a great one—but I wanted to speak about her as the person she was, not the role she played. While considering what to say, I thought of a seemingly unrelated event that had happened ten years before.

In 1993, I attended a dinner in Washington that honored President Nelson Mandela for his efforts to end hunger in Africa. At the end of the evening I had the pleasure of a few moments with this great man, where we shook hands. The kindness in his eyes and the warmth of his smile were palpable. Though it may sound strange, I could actually see light coming out of his eyes and mouth as he smiled. I felt as if we were the only two people in the world at that moment. It was very intimate.

The night before the funeral, as I thought about who my mother was as a human being, I realized that she was a best friend to all—her family, her neighbors, her co-workers, in fact, everyone she met. That was her stance. Because she was always being a best friend, naturally she was a great mother. What else is a great mother but the lifetime best friend of her children?

As I drove to the funeral the next morning, it suddenly hit me. Though they were different in color, ethnicity, religion, nationality, and gender, Nelson Mandela and my mother were nearly identical twins in spirit. The look of kindness in his eyes, the warmth of his smile, and the light pouring out of him were so familiar because I had already seen them thousands of times in the eyes and the smile of my mother. Both of these people were being best friends to everyone they met.

I was choked with emotion and humbled by my mother's greatness. All I could think of was that my mother was a person of greatness, no different from President Mandela, simply in a

different role. Both were being best friends to all—one on the home stage, the other on the world stage. Both played their roles magnificently.

It is not the role that someone plays that makes her a great person, though taking on a large role for the good of many can increase capacity and engender greatness. It is the essential quality—or being—of the person in whatever role she plays that makes her great or not. The French have a word for something small that is exquisite in every way. They call it *bijou*, a jewel. There is a cashier in a small supermarket in the Napa Valley who is a jewel. I have seen her on several visits. She is profoundly leading in job satisfaction, a rare commodity these days. She lights up with every customer. I have never seen her be any other way with anyone. No matter how many people are in her line, I wait, because what you get in her line is worth the wait.

One day I told the cashier that she is famous. She smiled and asked why. I said, "Because I talk about you and tell people that you are the happiest cashier in the world. When I mention you to people who live in this area, everyone knows who you are. You are as much of an attraction to me as any major winery in this valley. Now you are going to be in a book I am writing." She laughed and said, "I sure do love what I do." Most people would hear that statement as the result of her boss, her co-workers, her customers, salary, or environment. I know that it is not what she gets from her job. It is what she *brings* to it. In other words, it is her stand for her job and she could bring that stand anywhere she worked. It is a powerful stand that has given her a strategy for personal happiness. A useful piece of advice: if you are dissatisfied with your job, first consider what stand you have for it. You may discover that you need to change your stand more than you need to change jobs.

Since 1999, the Disney Corporation has been putting the national spotlight on teachers with their American Teacher Awards. These awards could rightly be called the Oscars of teaching. Major celebrities present the awards. The teachers are accurately presented as authentic leaders.

These teachers live in the everyday world of elementary and high schools. When you look at their lives, you see people leading with extraordinary heart, championing innovation, and inspiring their students to lives they would not otherwise have. They are a stand for empowering the next generation. Ultimately, these people will be far more important to millions of children and their families than any movie star or athlete ever could be. They are jewels.

You can measure your greatness by your ability to lead in any role you play. You can expand that role by expanding your own capacity in it or by expanding the number of people who are influenced by you. You can also take a new stand anytime you want by completing the stand you hold currently and using the power of your voice to create a new one. You can also add stands to the ones you already have, as long as they are in integrity with one another. The most important thing to remember is that you are not the role itself. You are not a thing. You are a verb, an experience. You are a human, being, someone who is being human. As such, you can reinvent who you are anytime you like.

Reinventing Your Stand

Though popular show-business performers are known for reinventing themselves every few years, what we normally see is someone presenting a new role for our entertainment and consumption, rather than someone becoming a new person. It is great to play new roles from time to time. Becoming someone new is entirely different.

The basis for all transformational experiences is a shift to a new location in being that changes fundamentally the way you see life and the opportunities available to you. The kind of reinvention that I am speaking about is an internal reorganization, arising from taking a stand that relocates you and requires you to think and act in brand-new ways. Choosing to be a leader in The New Feminine Principle is one such relocation.

To alter your being consciously and with deliberate intention has extraordinary power. People who are good at reinvention have the experience of living five or six discrete lives in one lifetime. Reinvention creates a feeling of freshness that is ageless, because you are (being) a new person when you change your starting point. Some common times when people reinvent themselves, though rarely as a conscious redesign, include:

- When they start school, or go from elementary to high school to college
- When they graduate from school and start a career
- When they marry and when they have children
- When they move to a different part of the country
- When they start a new job, get promoted, or leave a job
- When they change careers or start their own business
- In mid-life
- When they divorce or when a spouse dies
- When their children grow and up and leave home
- When they retire

How to Reinvent Yourself

The subject, methodology, and art of reinvention are discussions that could rightfully have a whole book devoted to them. I have listed below, in very simple form, eleven basic steps for reinventing yourself. I will use leadership in The New Feminine Principle as the core around which you are reorganizing yourself, though it could be anything you choose.

1. **Acknowledge and complete who you are being now.**

   Do the completion process on the answer to this question: "Who am I currently being in my life regarding leadership?" The first answer you get is usually the right one. If you get more than one answer, you can do more than one completion or use the answer that feels right to you.

2. **Take your stand for leadership.**

   Use the power of your voice and declare yourself a leader in The New Feminine Principle.

3. **Choose who you will be going forward.**

   Ask yourself, "Who do I need to be to fulfill this stand?" The answer to this question is the key to reinventing yourself. To be a leader in The New Feminine Principle, you may need to be "someone who keeps my word to myself," "someone who is well nourished emotionally," "someone who has a powerful voice for my desires," "someone who is kind to myself," or "someone who can have her visions realized." The number of answers to this question is unlimited. Pick the answer that sets you free.

4. **Do a ritual to welcome this leadership into yourself.**

   The power of invocation has been used throughout time to create the living presence of a particular quality or experience. The ritual should express your own personal creativity. It can be as long or short, simple or complex as you like. The important thing is that the ritual should speak to you emotionally. All rituals of invocation are meant to evoke an emotional response. This is the power of religious, political, business, and social rituals. They speak to the heart, not just the intellect.

5. **Make a list of things that will support your new way of being.**

   Choose the five most important things that will make you feel natural with the way of being that comes from your stand. I recommend you do this after you have spent some time with your appetite and desire. Let yourself want as much as you can from this stand. The information you get will be charged with turn-on and be that much more desirable to you. I recommend that you include in your five things a token, an announcement, two behaviors that you will do consistently for a month to activate this new being, and something that deeply touches your heart.

A *token* is a constant reminder of the new being that you are calling in. A token can be anything from a piece of jewelry to a shell you find on the beach. The cost is unimportant. The significance of the object is what counts. Give yourself a token and keep it around you.

Announcements are useful for letting people know they can expect something new. You can tell your closest friends or make an announcement, as graduates do, to dozens of people about what you have taken on. Be careful not to make your announcement to people who are cynical or negative. Make it to people who will understand and be responsive to what you are undertaking.

Consistent behaviors that activate new ways of being are important because they take what is new out of the idea stage and put it into practice. Behavioral psychologists say anything you think or practice for twenty-one to twenty-eight days becomes a habit. I recommend that you choose two things that are easy and practical. For example, you can make a list of things you want from being this new way and add a few items several times a week. You can also do the completion process every day about beliefs that empower or impede your stand. The behaviors do not have to be complicated (it's better if they are not). The most important aspect is consistency and repetition. It is better to do a behavior three times a week for four weeks than to do it five times in one day and then not at all for two weeks.

Something that deeply touches your heart is anything that speaks powerfully to you and confirms you are being this new way. For example, if you take a stand for being someone who leads in kindness, you can visit someone who is ill and needs cheering up. If your stand is to be leading in generosity, you can praise someone whose behavior you normally take for granted. What you do is less important than how you do it. Whatever it is, do it in a way that touches your heart.

6. **Identify opportunities to act in your new way of being.**
   Over the next thirty days, follow through on your list and see everything that happens as an opportunity to be this new way

you desire to be. Ask yourself, "Being a leader in (the new way), what is the appropriate action or interpretation to take at this moment?" Practice using every single experience during that time to confirm and reinforce your leadership. You have the power of interpretation, which is a profound power. Use it to see how everything contributes to your stand and your new way of being. Sometimes this requires being very creative.

For example, a friend of mine who wants to be a nightclub performer has a powerful stand that God is her best friend and everything that happens to her is for her good. For six months, one thing after the other went wrong. First her car broke down. Then her apartment flooded. The list went on and on. When I asked her how she was doing, she said, "I know this is God's way of making me strong. Every day I thank God for cleansing my spirit (her very powerful inter-pretation) and I keep reminding myself that I'll need to be strong and clear about myself to be in the public eye."

I attended her first public performance in a local nightclub. She was polished and was well received. Two days later, I visited her and saw a poster for her performance on her kitchen wall. Her face had been scratched out. When I asked her about it, she said, "A woman who lives in this apartment complex got jealous over my big break and defaced the poster. I'm leaving it on my kitchen wall to remind me that God wants me to be humble about success and to realize that not everyone needs to like me for me to be successful." This is a woman who is leading in interpreting and using every circumstance for her good. Clearly, God *is* her best friend because she says so and acts accordingly.

7. **Validate and appreciate every time you act on being consistent with your stand.**

Novices make mistakes. Do not criticize yourself for mistakes you make. That only impairs and delays the process. You do not have to get a score of 100 percent all the time to become who you want to be. Use jellybeans in a jar, stars on the refrigerator, or some other kidlike device to mark your wins. They work for kids. Because you were a kid once, they will work for you and allow you to have some fun in the process.

8. Be prepared for a turning point.

A sudden, often powerful choice point will occur. Expect and welcome it. This is the critical moment when, if you choose the new way of being, it becomes real for you. It is from this moment of choice that epiphany, *an illuminating moment or sudden new interpretation of the data*, occurs. For some, the choice point is a fearful experience because it takes them away from what is familiar; however, not everyone is afraid when it arrives, and some are wildly excited. You will be safe if you choose the new way of being and act accordingly.

A client of mine who had been a heavy smoker told me that twenty years ago, she took a stand for her health and threw her cigarettes away. She followed many of the recommendations for quitting smoking and was doing great until about three weeks later. "All of a sudden, I had the kind of craving for cigarettes that I can only imagine is like what heroine addicts have," she said. "I began to sweat. My body got very tense. I felt as if I were being possessed. It was agonizing. This went on for fifteen or twenty minutes until I got furious and hollered at the top of my lungs, 'You're going to have to kill me before I'll smoke another f****** cigarette.' I had no idea who I was talking to, but within a few moments everything stopped and I got very peaceful. I realized in that one moment that I would never be bullied into anything for the rest of my life. I've lived that way for the last twenty years. My kids call me The Rock."

9. Celebrate passing the choice point.

When you have passed the choice point and found yourself squarely in your new stand, acknowledge it by an act of celebration and gratitude. With any new creation—a child, a business, or a personal strategy—there is a "grand opening" that marks the new beginning and says you are open for business. Your celebration can be as private or public, as simple or elaborate as you like. The important thing is to mark the occasion by celebrating and offering heartfelt gratitude for the change.

10. Recognize new pathways.

Now that you are standing in a brand-new place, pay attention to new opportunities and choices. Also, notice and celebrate choices that are different from before.

The mind is a generalizing machine. As President Reagan so inelegantly stated, "If you've seen one redwood, you've seen them all." Your mind will try to compare what you are doing now to what you have done before in an attempt to make who you are now logically coherent with who you have been previously. It will repeat over and over, "Nothing is new. This is just like that." When it comes to recognizing objects, like chairs, this generalizing function is very useful. It is not so useful when it comes to recognizing yourself as someone brand-new.

It is important to recognize new pathways, opportunities, and experiences. They anchor your new way of being and validate it, so your mind will generalize from the new pathways, rather than the old ones.

11. Actively inquire into your stand.

Find out what it will take to be masterful with it and pick people to support you. Some new ways of being require several years of intensive inquiry and may require training, coaching, and partnership to achieve them. The most masterful dancers cultivate who they are being as dancers for years and practice every single day, often with teachers for different kinds of dance or levels of skill. This keeps their mastery fresh.

It is vital to know that, while you are responsible for the life you want, you do not have to go it alone. To pick people who can help you become who you want to become and to surround yourself with people on similar journeys are two of the secrets of sustainability.

You can do a number of things in the company of others that will contribute to the quality of your stand for leadership, including the following:

- Do completions and practice taking stands with friends.
- Call one another and express gratitude.

- Begin a program of reinvention with others and all do it together.
- Practice with others ways of thinking and speaking about your stand and of taking effective action on it.
- Do the State of Nourishment Survey with your partner, pick an area that you want to nourish, and have your partner support you.
- Use a mix of people with different points of view to increase your appetite and desire. It is perfectly fine to add what others want to the list of what you want. There is plenty to go around.

Women are natural in circles. Use circles of women to support your stands and who you are being by empowering one another together.

One Woman's Reinvention

Jane was a woman who was driven by her commitments. She had a schedule jammed full of meetings, projects, and events that kept her going at a phenomenal pace. When she completed this way of being (driven), she cried for more than fifteen minutes and said she was exhausted, but didn't know what to do to stop. She envisioned herself leading a life that is a pleasure. When she asked who she needed to be to live a life that is a pleasure, she discovered that she needed to be someone who is really in touch with her appetite and desire.

Jane took a weekend away and did a ceremony at the ocean. She took an old picture of herself at work, ripped it up, and threw it in the ocean. She found a sand dollar on the beach that she decided was the token of her new way of being. Then she went back to her hotel room and "gave myself a long and languorous evening of pleasure to welcome in the new me."

During that evening, she decided that she would do at least one completion a day for a month on various topics related to pleasure. She promised to add to her list of appetites in as many different areas as she could, at least three times a week. She also decided that she would do at least one thing every day for a month that was solely for her pleasure.

Around day ten, Jane started to get upset. She had gone overboard—as she often did. I advised her to take a day off from her action plan and spend some time with her best friend. I encouraged her to ask her friend to listen while she talked about everything. I also encouraged Jane to express as much gratitude as possible for what had already happened, and to have an evening of romance and sex with her husband. These sound like easy assignments, but when you are this overloaded, pleasure is the last thing on your mind.

On day twelve, Jane started again, this time more slowly. She did a completion on her current ability to pace herself. She felt better. She spent a day with her mother just hanging out. She said it touched her heart to go through a day with her mother with no agenda. It was unlike anything she had ever done with her. Things went more smoothly.

Around day twenty-three, Jane reached a turning point. Out of the blue, her company offered her a promotion with more responsibility and a move to another state. After three days of anxiety and debate, she realized that more responsibility was exactly what she did not need to live her life as a pleasure. She had no appetite for the new job.

She turned down the promotion—something that would have been completely unthinkable to her before. I encouraged her to tell her superior why she was turning down the promotion and if there were a chance, to voice her appetite and desire for the job that would be her complete pleasure. Her boss thanked her for her honesty.

Jane was asked twice by higher-ups in her company to reconsider. She felt that to take the job would be a real compromise. There were subtle insinuations that if Jane did not take the job she was at a dead end in her career. She laughed and said she would start her own company if they fired her or tried to put her in a dead-end slot. She stayed true to her promises.

Two months later, she telephoned and sounded more excited than I had ever heard her. She reminded me of the conversation we had when she said she would start her own company. "Last night," she nearly shouted, "I realized that starting my own company is exactly what I should do, not because they might fire me, but because I have secretly had that dream for several years. It would be a huge turn-on for me and I am ready."

The kind of reinvention that Jane experienced is a natural part of living, though most people go through the process unconsciously or haphazardly. What may make adolescence hard for children is that they know they are changing and need to form a new identity (take a new stand) but no one teaches them any coherent way to do that. Currently, we live with a stand to "get through it as best we can." One of my godchildren said that he thought reinvention should be a class that every student is required to take. Indeed, such a class would be invaluable, but first the teachers would have to learn to do it themselves.

The Turning Point

When you select less, you get less. When you compromise, you get only some of what you want or you get something that you did not really want as a substitute for what you really wanted. I love chocolate. People used to tell me carob tasted just as good. Carob is good, but not if you want chocolate. If you want a life that is completely satisfying, it is important not to pick things that are less than satisfying to you.

Many years ago, while still a psychotherapist, I worked with a man named Dennis who was having problems in his career. He was an environmental specialist working for a large engineering firm. Dennis was married to a wonderful woman who was very successful in business. They had three beautiful children and a lifestyle that would be the envy of many people. Still, Dennis was not happy and felt that he had lost his way in life.

Though I did not call the process reinvention then, I worked intensively with Dennis to open up his voice and talk about his real appetites and desires, and to see his life from a different perspective. I put him on a program to get more turned on and told him to make lists of what he would like and who he would like to be. Dennis dutifully made lists and reported what was on them each week. Nothing seemed to be happening.

In one of our sessions, I asked him if there had ever been a period in his life when he felt happy and turned on all the time. "One stands out," he said. "When I was young man, I joined the Peace Corps and was assigned to Malaysia. Though it was difficult at times and unfamiliar, the year I spent there was one of the best of my life. I knew I was making a real contribution to those people and would have been happy to live my whole life that way. Working on projects for a big company that only cares about its profits is the last thing I thought I would ever do." It was easy to hear that Dennis's true stand, the one that set him free, was "I am making a big difference in the quality of people's lives."

Over the next few weeks, the tension between his hopes and his situation increased. One day, Dennis announced that he still had the address of his mentor from the Peace Corps and was thinking about contacting him and talking things over. I encouraged him. The next time we met, Dennis looked like a different human being. He was beaming.

"I called my mentor. He told me there is an opening for a person with my talents in Indonesia. I would spend a year working on a five-year plan for housing that would have enormous impact on the people. The only problem," he said, "is that this opportunity is creating a crisis in my family."

Dennis's wife, Karen, was unhappy about the prospect of living in a developing country. She worried about their children's health and education, her own career, and a host of other potential problems. The turning point had arrived.

After two months, Dennis reported that he had to go or die. He said, "I told Karen that if I miss this opportunity, though I love her and the kids, I won't be any good to them or anyone else. Finally she agreed that I should go, but she doesn't want to relocate our family. We worked out a schedule of calls and visits back to the States and my whole family will spend the summer with me next year in Indonesia." I have seldom seen a human being radiate more happiness.

During the next twelve months, I got updates from Dennis or Karen. The visits went as planned. The family had a summer adventure in Indonesia that they will remember all their lives. When Dennis returned, Karen and he and I had dinner to celebrate. Over dessert, Karen told me something remarkable. She said, "I realized during this year that the real reason I was so opposed to Dennis going was that I felt dependent on Dennis to fill in all the areas where I thought I couldn't make it. When he went for his dream, I discovered that I have everything it takes right here inside me. If he hadn't gone, I wouldn't know that." Through his unwillingness to compromise his stand to make a big difference in the quality of other people's lives, Dennis made a big difference in the life of his own wife. Fifteen years later, Dennis and Karen are still together and doing well.

Terra Incognita: Into the Future

On ancient maps, there were territories that were labeled *terra incognita*, literally, "the unknown land." Drawings of dragons and other fantastical creatures were put in these areas to indicate that whatever these lands held was beyond current imagining. No one would ever know these lands until someone had the courage to explore them and discover their secrets.

In the modern world, there are few good examples of leadership based on The New Feminine Principle. We live in a world where the dominator version of The Masculine Principle is in full power, but The New Feminine Principle is still terra incognita.

This is a challenging notion to come to grips with, but you must if you take on leadership in the way that I am proposing. Who you are as a conscious leader in The New Feminine Principle is not who you are now plus leadership plus skill in The Feminine Principle as it now stands. You will become someone brand new, because you will have reanimated your spirit, gained your voice, opened your appetite and desire fully, and learned to master reality by having the power to change a model that you thought was gender based and, therefore, immutable. This is called personal evolution. It is the ultimate invention.

When you have gained your voice, who knows what you will declare? When you have reclaimed your full appetite and desire, who knows what you will truly desire? When you have completed beliefs and experiences that you have been carrying for decades, who knows what will get freed up in you? When you ask the spirit of leadership in you for guidance about whom to be, who knows what it will say?

There is profound joy in something new, as you can see with babies. This same joy can be had over and over as you express your leadership in new, unexpected ways and emerge as a leader in your own, unique right, as the terra incognita within you gets explored, charted, and mapped.

For Joan Holmes, in her work to end world hunger, the world in which hunger is ended is definitely not this world plus the end of hunger. At this very moment, there are sufficient resources to feed every single person, and technology is available that could allow us to feed many times more. What is missing is the collective political and social will to make ending hunger our priority. We have to evolve as human beings, as a world, to the point where we demand that everyone be fed. We have to see what we have not been able to see before. We have to voice new priorities about money, our laws, whom we elect, and what we expect them to do. The consciousness of the world opens person-by-person or it doesn't open at all. When enough of us demand the world we want by being leaders in our own right, we will get public leaders who demand that, too.

What we are up against is the need for a radical shift in consciousness, an epiphany, a new mindset or model, a breakthrough in being, a leap forward in ourselves—not more solutions based on where we currently stand. If ever there were a critical need for invention, it is now. As you take a stand and invent a new strategy for your life that grants greatness, you add mass to the desire for a new stand in the world at large.

Human beings live with a pretense that they know how it will be when something new is created or comes into play. If you had lived in 1903, could you have predicted landing on the moon from the Wright Brothers' several-minute flight at Kitty Hawk? Did you predict in 1980 that in 2005, you would carry your own personal telephone with you and that people anywhere on earth could contact you anywhere you went using this device? In your own life, did you at age fourteen imagine who you would be and what would interest you at age thirty-five? As life grows, it evolves and changes in wonderful ways that enable or compel us to be completely different people from anyone we were before.

At the moment, we have millions of people praying for peace. Every single faction seems to have a way to get there and an idea of how peace will look. In actuality, no one can predict how we will get there—if we ever do. Peace may have nothing at all to do with what we think from where we are standing, because we will need to stand in a brand-new place to see the solutions we need. As Gandhi so powerfully said, we will have to be—one by one—the world we want, for it to come into reality.

There is no possible way to imagine what will happen when thirty million women (one percent of females worldwide) or one hundred million women (three percent) find the voice of their leadership in The New Feminine Principle. Who knows what

declarations they will make, what stands they will take, and
what global conversations they will initiate? Who knows what
unprecedented, miraculous developments will come from feminine leadership? Who can honestly say they know how men will
react? If men in the United States are any indication, millions of
men might jump ship on the dominator model and choose one
that has more kindness in it, as more and more younger men are
doing now.

There is no single answer to the question, "What would life as
a leader in The New Feminine Principle be like?" The answer is
a path to follow—a living investigation into a future that opens
as you walk into it. You make critical distinctions as you go, looking at life through the lens of ongoing leadership, a state that is
barely imaginable until you are there.

The answer to the question, "Being a leader in The New Feminine Principle, what is the most appropriate action to take at this
moment?" changes from one moment and from one situation
to the next. The opportunities and challenges you will have and
the ways you will respond to your own conscious leadership are
potentially as different from your current opportunities and challenges as Kansas was from Oz.

The Individuality of Leadership

Things that are mass produced are less valuable than handcrafted
items because they lack individuality and life energy. When a human being touches anything, there is a transfer of energy. When
you make something by hand, the spiritual value is the investment of energy and personal idiosyncrasy you added. What you
make has life because you put your life force into it. Similarly,
what you make of your own life is only as good as the life force
you put into it.

We live with a belief from the dominator model that life is
cheap. When you see photos of a sea of humanity walking down

the streets of Hong Kong or London, it is easy to think that human beings are mass produced and can easily be replaced or exchanged. Nothing could be farther from the truth.

The truth is that we were made one by one as a unique mix of physical, mental, and spiritual qualities provided by our parents in an act that is as personal as it gets. There is almost no chance of any of us ever being duplicated again. Each and every human being is a handcrafted masterpiece. People who cook from scratch portray this principle beautifully. Though they might have cooked a particular dish dozens of times, each time it has subtle variations and differences that make you feel as if you are tasting it for the very first time.

You contain a unique blueprint of spirit and form handed down to you through the bodies of millions of people—your ancestors—who expressed The Feminine Principle in the great mystery of sexual connection. The combination of the shape of your head, plus whether you like peas, plus the parts of the world that call to you, and thousands more qualities are unique to you alone. Even identical twins have different points of view, because they cannot literally stand in the same place at the same time.

Do idiosyncrasies or imperfections make you less valuable? No. They increase your value and create your individuality.

My former wife, Diane, is an expert quilt maker. She has taught me many useful distinctions about quilt making that are also applicable to life at large. One day my mother called to tell Diane that a woman in her neighborhood had discovered many handmade quilt tops. They were in her grandmother's cedar chest, which had been filled with mothballs, so they were in good shape. By the look of their patterns, they had probably been made around the time of the Civil War. The woman was selling them to neighbors and friends for fifty dollars each—the bargain of a lifetime! Because I was planning to visit my mother, Diane and I agreed that I should look at the quilt tops and buy whatever I thought was great.

A week later I was in the woman's basement. As promised, the quilt tops were in good shape. Having picked four quilt tops, I noticed that there were tiny splatters of brown stains on two of the quilts. I called Diane and told her about the stains and asked for her opinion about whether they were worth buying. She got excited and said, "Bill, those are chewing tobacco stains. Women often chewed tobacco while quilting and sometimes when they spit it out, tiny stains got on the quilts. The stains actually make the quilt more valuable because they identify the quilt as being from that era and authenticate it." All of a sudden, the tobacco stains were charming.

The word *perfection* means "ideal." The important word here is *idea*. *Ideal* is just an idea about the way things should be. When you let go of needing things or people to be a certain way and are able to get nourishment from them just the way they are, then you can enjoy them and they have the freedom to be perfectly themselves. They do not have to change anything to be of value. They can be perfectly who they are. When you let go of having to be a certain way in order to be able to find leadership in yourself, you have the freedom to be perfectly yourself. You also have the freedom to change in ways that give you more, anytime you want, without the pressure of trying to get it right.

The form that a life of leadership in The New Feminine Principle takes will be different for each and every human being because we are handcrafted, not mass produced. Who you will become and what you will do are unique to you. Leadership comes in many diverse forms and all of them are good and useful. What people who have chosen leadership have in common is the shared experience of the pleasure and power of that leadership, not the form it takes. So enjoy being a leader and pick a form that best expresses you.

In Conclusion

We have been ruthlessly indoctrinated with the injunction against playing with ourselves. Though you might have learned this injunction in connection with your sexuality, the mind, being a generalizing machine, will extend that injunction to every area of your life, till finally you don't play with your joy, your money, your family, your job, your spirit, or your leadership.

One way to look at evolution itself is to see everything as nature evolving in a gigantic, cosmic act of play. Nature creates millions of new forms. Some of them flourish and some of them don't. So what? To paraphrase Shakespeare, maybe the play's the thing.

Use the wise advice of Jesus to "Become as a child again …." Play with your leadership. Give yourself the freedom to throw away what you thought might work but didn't. Change games whenever you want. Put away one game and pull out another. You do not need anyone's permission but your own.

Honestly, we have absolutely no way of knowing what real leadership in The New Feminine Principle will look like when five million people are leading in it publicly. They will have values in common, but my guess is that the style each person creates will be a unique design, her own personal thumbprint. What is clear is that if you are looking for a recipe for leadership in The New Feminine Principle, you will miss out on one of the greatest opportunities you could possibly have—to create yourself as a leader in your own style, standing for a future that is not like anything we have had before.

My own conclusion is that to be leading in The New Feminine Principle is the most powerful expression of responsibility for yourself and your world that is currently available. To take the stand that all life is connected, to see that in each life all life is represented, to embody these principles, and to cooperate as fully as you can with life around you—these are the most powerful expressions of enlightened self-interest you can make. Within this model, you have more of what you want for yourself and the world has more of what it wants from you, namely to have life continue, to sustain itself, and to grow and evolve.

Now we are full circle. You know that we live in models of reality that have enormous power. You know that The Feminine Principle as it stands is a model. More importantly, you know that any model can be changed or a new model invented anytime you want. Use your power! Open the power of your voice and take a stand for The New Feminine Principle that gives you wholeness. Grant yourself the power of authorship, which is real authority. Take the power of your turn-on off its leash and let it lead you. Increase your capacity till you have the power to desire the full greatness that God has in mind for you. Celebrate and be grateful for the opportunity to be alive. Invent a new you anytime you want. Play with your life and have fun with it. We desperately need to know what that ongoing celebration looks like if we want a world of happiness, so sign yourself up as a pioneering citizen of a new world. Real feminine power is the power to invite, magnetize, inspire, and empower as many people as you can to come to the party. From this power, the future we all desire can be created and realized.

Epilogue: Hunger Is Ending. Your Leadership Is Required

O━━⚓

In the last 29 years, there has arisen a worldwide movement of people who are committed to the sustainable end of hunger—a problem which primarily affects our world's women and children. The Hunger Project is both a movement and an organization, whose mission is not to provide relief and food. There are many effective organizations that serve this need. The Hunger Project's mandate is to figure out, step by step, what it will take to bring about a world where hungry people have a real opportunity to end their own hunger.

According to international organizations such as the United Nations, activating the voice of women and empowering them to act on their voice are *the* crucial elements for ending hunger and reconstructing the world in which we live. As a matter of fact, the world we live in will be a completely different place when women find their voice, because that voice includes relatedness, a larger sense of family, the importance of our long-term sustainability, real investment in all our children, and dozens of other key variables that, taken together, are the best index of the quality of life for all human beings.

One Woman's Empowerment

Through these 29 years, one woman, Joan Holmes, has stood at the head of this global movement along with countless thousands of women and men who share her vision (though it might be more appropriate to say that Joan has stood at the *heart* of the movement to end hunger). Like many great leaders, Joan did not come from a background of wealth and privilege. She was simply a woman who, in 1977, chose to bring into existence a project whose goal was to make the end of hunger an idea whose time had come. In doing so, she found the true, evolving nature of her greatness. In fact, you could say that The Hunger Project is the expression of one woman finding her voice for the end of hunger.

Joan has made it her personal mandate to continually identify the beliefs and attitudes that prevent us from having the world we want, by first identifying them in herself. Then she systematically completes these beliefs and begins a process of inquiry into the truth that will take us into a future where hunger has ended. When she has discovered the truth of the next step into that future, then and only then, she takes a stand for that truth and asks the people of The Hunger Project around the world to act on it.

I have had the great privilege of witnessing Joan do this dozens of times over the years as she opens a path to a world that no one has ever seen. It is a miraculous process and a brilliant demonstration of leadership by empowerment. She does it over and over and will until hunger ends.

Here are some of the beliefs that The Hunger Project has completed and moved beyond:

- Hunger is inevitable.
- There are no solutions to the problem.
- There is insufficient food or resources to solve the problem.
- Women are inferior.
- Poor people are stupid or lazy.
- People from different cultures or religions will never cooperate.

These and other beliefs are losing their power to hold hunger in place. What is arising, instead, is the leadership, action, and results of millions of women in the poorest countries.

Leadership Everywhere in Everyone

Through The Hunger Project, Joan has empowered women and men—in both the developed and developing worlds—to activate their stand and their voice for the end of hunger, and to take action consistent with their commitment. Now, after nearly 30 years, there are thousands of people like Joan Holmes around the world, looking into and completing their own limiting beliefs and taking action on the world they want. In a world where people are empowered to act on the end of hunger or any other important issue—whoever or wherever they are—one powerful result is that an abundance of real leadership emerges in harmony with the idea, "Think globally, act locally."

Hunger is ending. Did you know that in the last 30 years the number of people who die from hunger has dropped 75 percent, from 28 million to 7 million a year? This is not to say that 7 million deaths a year from hunger is acceptable. It is not, but it certainly is real progress. Has any newspaper or TV show let you know that there are Millennium Development Goals with targets to reduce poverty, region by region, by 50 percent in the next 10 years? Probably not.

As Joan Holmes has said so powerfully, the world in which hunger has ended is not the world we know now minus hunger. It is a world where every person has the opportunity for a great life. That world is emerging right now.

There are many ways to lead in ending hunger, such as voting, sending petitions to political leaders, volunteering, raising money, and raising consciousness about hunger. There is also the issue of the spiritual hunger that lives in people in the developed world, which is a mirror of physical hunger. Your leadership and your voice add to leadership globally, though I know it is sometimes difficult to see that right in your own backyard. You co-create the world we all want—including a world where everyone is nourished and has a chance for a productive life—by activating the voice of your own leadership and taking a stand for the world you want. Frankly, when you have activated your voice and leadership, no one (not even you) knows what contribution you might make.

The Final Hurdle

Since 1996, The Hunger Project has made the empowerment of women its primary focus and is championing it in the villages of the developing world and the halls of world power. The dominator view of reality continues, however, because women and the men who champion them have not raised their voices to demand strongly enough a new reality in which equality and partnership are the rule. Billions of women are forced or conditioned to remain silent in the face of their dreams, of what they know is right and good, and of their own promise to themselves that life will be better for their children, many of whom are the actual victims of hunger. Martin Luther King said that the real tragedy of Nazi Germany were the decent Germans who knew what was happening and kept silent. The silence is the killer.

As you know, the lack of voice is not a problem "over there" somewhere; it exists right here in us as well. There is only one place where voice occurs and that is in you. When you open your voice by telling the truth about your desire and take a stand for the fulfillment of that desire in yourself and the world around you, you personally create a new world. From there, there is only one thing to do: step into it by acting on your stand.

It's All About *You*

As the sage Confucius said, "The journey of a thousand miles begins with a single step." Nobel Peace Prize laureate Betty Williams, tired of the killings in her neighborhood, started knocking on her neighbors' doors and asking them to demand peace.

From her simple neighborly actions, the Northern Ireland Peace Movement was born. Similarly, Africa Prize laureate Wangari Maathai planted trees in her own backyard and encouraged other women to do the same. From that simple action, the Green Belt Movement, which has planted ten million trees and helped restore the ecosystem of Kenya, was born. Let's not forget Mary Kay Ash who, tired of the way she and other women were being treated in business, borrowed $5,000 and founded a cosmetics company that has made more American women financially successful than any other single business.

Tens of thousands of women, who were elected village leaders for the first time and trained by The Hunger Project to be effective in their new roles, have taken the step into the future they want. Seventeen million of the world's poorest women in Bangladesh, who borrowed $100 or less from the Grameen Bank to start their own businesses, have taken the step. None of these women is essentially different from you. Everything that makes them great and allows them to take that first step lives in you. That's really good news.

Feel your desire and find your voice, take a stand, and *act* right where you are. Then you are a co-creator of your world—a world leader in your own right.

(For more information on this worldwide movement, contact The Hunger Project at www.thp.org or 212-251-9100.)